Advance Praise for Moving to the Center of the Bed

"A compelling and inspiring journey of self-discovery. Weinstein displays immense courage, wisdom, and authenticity through profoundly challenging times. Her candor and eloquence will remain with you long after you've read *Moving to the Center of the Bed*."

Pam Bradley, Former Administrator,
Silverado Senior Living, Encinitas, California

"A courageous journey into the center of life itself. Sheila's reflection on her husband's rare terminal illness and excruciating loss of self is beautifully juxtaposed with the story of her own profound healing and reclaiming of self. Her loving family, her creativity in the form of writing and music, and her spiritual connection are the angels who accompany her into the darkness and out again into the light. By learning to create a life alone Sheila has gained not just her authentic self but also a very real connection to the world."

Gail Straub, author of
Returning to My Mother's House* and *The Rhythm of Compassion

"Sheila Weinstein's raw emotion transports the reader to a place that grants them permission to embrace their own emotional journeys. Never before have I been exposed to writing that so honestly exemplifies the roller coaster that is dealing with loss while trying to learn to live alone after a partnership of many years. Sheila teaches us how to love, how to be honest with ourselves and our feelings, and how to always see the light at the end of the tunnel."

Shevonne Farrell, MSW

"Powerful and poetic, Sheila Weinstein's unforgettable memoir walks its way into the sinews of your soul and leaves indelible images of a woman's midlife journey towards being and becoming anew. *Moving to the Center of the Bed* is a beautifully crafted story of bittersweet memories, triumph amidst tragedy, aging and aloneness. The author allows us to live inside her determined spirit as life moves her from place to place in search of a home for her heart and another for a dying husband. Weinstein pushes past fear and pain to weave an undeniably poignant tale that will leave you breathless with its clarity and candor. It is truly a story to be loved, shared, treasured and read many times over."

Dorothy Randall Gray,
author of *Soul Between The Lines: Freeing Your Creative Spirit Through Writing*

"Sheila Weinstein's voice is true and unique. Her story is both her own, and in many ways, one that resonates as that of many. *Moving to the Center of the Bed* is a wise and beautifully wrought memoir that will long linger in every reader's mind."

Jonathon Lazear, author of *The Man Who Mistook His Job for a Life*

Moving to the Center of the Bed

The Artful Creation of a Life Alone

Sheila Weinstein

CENTER OF THE BED PUBLISHING
New York, New York

"How to Eat Alone", from SEASONAL RIGHTS by Daniel Halpern, copyright © 1979, 1980, 1981, 1982 by Daniel Halpern. Used by permission of Viking Penguin, a division of Penguin Group (USA) Inc.

Center of the Bed Publishing
www.centerofthebed.com

Weinstein, Sheila.

Moving to the center of the bed : the artful creation of a life alone / Sheila Weinstein. —New York, N.Y. : Center of the Bed Pub., c2009.

p. ; cm.

ISBN: 978-09820822-0-1

1. Women—Life skills guides. 2. Divorced women—Life skills guides. 3. Single women—Life skills guides. 4. Widows—Life skills guides. 5. Loss (Psychology) 6. Grief. I. Title.

HQ2037 .W45 2009   2008936344
305.4—dc22   0812

Printed in the United States of America

Cover and interior design by To The Point Solutions
www.tothepointsolutions.com

Dedicated to:

Barbara James, who showed me the way and then walked beside me, righting me when I stumbled. Without her caring and loving presence in my life I am certain this book would never have come to be.

My children and grandchildren—Bruce, Lizzie, Rachel, Carlee, and Sammy—my dearest ones.

George, my husband of fifty years, whose gentle love and kindness will live within me always.

And, to all women who have found themselves suddenly alone and struggling to move to the center of their own beds. I hope what you find in this book will comfort you and give you cause to know that you will get through, and, yes, that you will even be happy again. Most of all that you are definitely not alone.

Contents

Contents

Contents

Preface

The chicken sizzles in the pan. My favorite
. . . seasoned, floured, and fried by my own hand.
I look out the window next to the stove. It is early
winter. Darkness has come on quickly, revealing an underlying
beauty of blinking lights in this granite sea. I have come to love
this city with the power of a foster child finally adopted. This
small kitchen, this small apartment, this grand view, is home.
And I wonder at the strangeness of that. A small stuffed-full
flat, where I am finally content . . . after a lifetime of large and
many-roomed homes . . . never feeling at peace . . . always
worried that I had it too good . . . that something terrible
would happen . . . the unexpected . . . and I was not prepared.
And the worst did happen . . . the unexpected . . . and I was
not prepared . . . and I had to start from the beginning . . . to
do the work I had never done . . . to find myself . . . and to
come to this day and to this place that is finally . . . home.

Acknowledgments

My deepest thanks . . .

To Jonathon Lazear, Christi Cardenas, and the Lazear Literary Agency, who had such confidence in me and my work, and who helped me find the shape of this book. I will always be grateful to you.

To Caroline Pincus, an astute editor, who became a loving friend who cried and laughed with me; and above all, encouraged me to write the book I wanted to write.

To Mary Jo Zazueta, my book designer, for her creative skill and patience with the most hands-on-client she has probably ever had.

To my dear friends who stayed by my side through my personal storm and who never wavered in their support and encouragement of me and of my writing—Paula Scardamalia, Jen Ortiz, Calla Cordova, Marlene Kandel, Jerry Ray, Phillipa Brinck, Shevonne Farrell, Pam Bradley, and Phyllis Rowland.

To Lorena Contera and Vangie Staley, whose loving care of my husband allowed me to sleep at night.

To my New York City writing friends, Mingmei Yip and Esta Fischer, for their astute commentary and friendship.

Acknowledgments

To Hannelore Hahn and the International Women's Writing Guild for telling me in 1991 that they welcomed all writers with or without portfolios. I might have stayed in my writing room and never allowed my scribbles to be seen.

To my sweet dog, Pooh, who continues to teach me about patience, loyalty, and how to be really naughty and still be loved to pieces.

To my doormen, Frank, Ray, George, and Vinny, to whom I come home every day and night and who welcomed me back with such gentle humanity from those difficult trips I made to the West Coast to see my husband. They have become family.

To the Body Tuning Studio—Shmuel Tatz, Viktor Jeriomenko, Valery Kovalenko, and Irina Goerke—whose kindness and skill keep me in shape to write, play the piano, and move around in my life.

To Tim Deep, my computer guru and website designer, for his patience and expertise with electronically challenged me.

To Drs. Helen Hecht, Marjorie McMaster, and Lorraine Chrisomalis, for listening compassionately to my heart and not only my symptoms.

To David Price and Richard Brock, friends forever, confidants, boosters, and to whom I owe whatever I do know about how to keep myself solvent.

To Robert Lee and his gentle art of keeping me focused.

To Amy Cantor, for her compassionate love, and to Tim Cantor, for his gifted art that keeps me believing, even on the darkest of nights.

Introduction

After forty-two years of marriage, my husband was gone without a goodbye. Several years ago, George was diagnosed with Pick's Disease, a fronto/temporal lobe dementia. A practicing ophthalmologist, he was sixty-four years old.

To the end of my life, I will remember the neurologist showing us the results of my husband's MRI. As he slid the films onto the illuminated screen, the doctor pointed to what looked like black holes in my husband's brain and gave us the clinical description of the disease and the symptoms that fit exactly my husband's recent puzzling behavior, the reason I had brought him to the Mayo Clinic in Jacksonville, Florida, for diagnosis.

I began to shiver in the small, frigid cubicle that looked like every other cubicle on every other floor in every building of the Clinic. I wrapped my arms around myself as the doctor with the soft accented voice droned on with the precision of a well-oiled machine. I felt dislocated in time and space, as if in a surreal movie. Of all the catastrophes I had ever envisioned befalling my husband or me . . . heart disease . . . cancer . . . a plane crash . . . I had never imagined dementia. But here it was in graphic detail. I could barely take it in.

Pointing to my husband's MRI, the doctor said, "The frontal and temporal lobes of the brain are being eroded. That's what the dark spaces tell us. That is what is causing the dementia. These films, plus the cognitive tests we've done, and the observations you've given us, Mrs. Weinstein, all bear that out. *Dementia* is a broad term. There are many forms of it. In your husband's case, the symptoms fit the diagnosis of probable Pick's Disease. I say *probable* because there is no way to know exactly until . . . autopsy."

My heart froze. Autopsy? Wait. Wait. What was this man saying? It can't be . . . not George.

George stood and looked closely at his MRI, his face impassive. Then he turned and sat down again.

"George?" I took his hand.

"Yes?"

"Are you okay?"

"Sure." He smiled and picked up a magazine.

I was stunned. I looked at the doctor.

"That is the nature of this disease. If there is a gift, it is that there is an inability to comprehend that there is anything wrong . . . or different. It is not the same as Alzheimer's disease where often the patient is very aware at first."

"Oh, God. I never heard of this. I'm a doctor's wife, and I never heard of this. Are you certain?"

"It's a rare disease. Many doctors haven't heard of it either, and that's why it is often misdiagnosed as, say, depression or other things. And yes, I'm certain. Unfortunately I have seen too many cases just like your husband's. I've also gone over his findings with my faculty. We are all in agreement."

Then came the details of the anatomy of the disease, the lack of medication or ability to cure, and its slow but inevitable progression towards death. With each spoken word I felt life as I had known it slide into the great black hole. I looked at George. Tall, elegant, beautifully dressed George. But he wasn't George and hadn't been George for a very long time.

I was hypnotized by the doctor's rote repetition of what to me was completely foreign. What the doctor was describing in grim detail was an illness that almost defied understanding . . . not cells going berserk . . . not the breakdown of the most powerful muscle in the body . . . overworked and overfed . . . but a wasting away of a brain that controlled every function in his body. Everything that made my husband who he was would soon be gone. I put my hands over my face. George was going to die. Sturdy, strong, indestructible George was going to die. And not easily, not gently . . . but by losing himself in pieces . . . everything he was, everything he knew. I heard a long, howling scream deep inside myself. When it stopped, I asked the question, quietly.

"How long?"

"It's difficult to say. We used to say two to eight years; but we were proved wrong. It may be a lot longer."

This was not happening. These were supposed to be the best years. Freedom, no responsibilities. This was all wrong. All wrong.

I turned to George and took his hand. He looked up from his magazine and smiled. He had no idea what was happening to him. I looked deeply into his beautiful green and trusting eyes and swore a silent oath to him and to myself that I would always take care of him, that he would never lack for anything and that I would never let him down. But deep within me I felt a kind of fear I had never before experienced.

"There's one more important thing I want to discuss with both of you," the doctor continued. "Dr. Weinstein must close his practice immediately."

Of course. Of course. I knew it. But how to ingest it? George had wanted to be a doctor since the age of twelve, when he wrote to the dean of a medical school to find out what he would have to do in his life to accomplish his goal. I had known George most of my life, and most of his. I'd been with him through medical school, internship, residency, and all of his academic appointments. And in the few minutes it had taken for the neurologist to give me his diagnosis, it had all ended. I wanted to beat my fists against the wall. I wanted to yell at the doctor, "No, no . . . he can't!" But, I was mute as tears ran down my face.

The doctor handed me a box of tissues and then looked at George. "Dr. Weinstein, you are going to have to close your practice."

George shook his head and said, "No. I'm not going to do that."

The doctor's voice became stern. "Dr. Weinstein. You have a serious problem and you must not see patients anymore."

I wanted to tell him to shut up . . . just shut up. Who did he think he was talking to?

"No. I won't do that," George said.

"Dr. Weinstein . . . I don't want to have to . . ."

I couldn't take another minute of his badgering. Did the brilliant neurologist think that George was going to agree to give up a career of forty-five years because he asked him to? Did he not, just a moment before, say that George couldn't understand any of this?

"Stop it, doctor." I was abrupt, bordering on rude. "It isn't going to happen here. I'll take care of it."

"Mrs. Weinstein. He must!"

"Yes, I KNOW!" I didn't want to be nasty. But I was hanging on by my eyelashes. "I said I'd take care of it."

"Please . . . immediately." The doctor wouldn't let it go. "And also . . . your husband should not be driving anymore."

That, too. Of course the doctor was right. Bit by bit the world was falling in around us, though George seemed hardly to notice.

"All right, then. Do you have any other questions?" the doctor said.

I shook my head no.

"Well, then, I'll see you back in a year." He stood and pulled the MRI from the screen, slid it into its envelope and handed it to me. He shook George's hand as if they were colleagues who had just discussed a patient. Then he shook my hand.

"Goodbye, doctor. Thank you." I said, which I wondered about later. Courtesy aside, what in the world was I thankful for? For learning the horrible truth of a cruel disease that had already begun to take away the man I had known and loved for most of my life? For telling me, without telling me, that my husband and I would not walk together into the orange sunset of our years? That George would soon forget his entire life, his stellar career, our children, and me? And that I would be left to remember as I faced the rest of my life alone?

When George and I were out in the hallway, he reached for my hand. I looked at him and tried to imagine the effect the doctor's words had had on him. But, true to what I had just been told about the disease and the emotional disconnection it brought, George turned to me and said, "So, where do you want to go for dinner?"

If I had ever felt alone, it paled by comparison to what I was feeling as we entered the elevator. Panic and shock made me dry-mouthed as we exited the Clinic and walked to our car, the click of my heels echoing in the cavernous parking garage. How could this happen? How could such a brilliant man fall prey to a brain-wasting disease? My husband, who had spent his life in service to his patients, who cared so much for their well-being, would soon be in need of the ultimate in care himself. Why? Why? Why? And would I be able to care for him? What about money? How much did we have? How much did we owe? And, if there came a time when I could not care for him, where would he go? Where would I go? I already knew in dreadful detail what was going to happen to him. But what would happen to me without him?

"I'll drive. You take a little rest," I said, expecting protest. George never liked the way I drive.

"Okay," he said.

My hand shook as I put the key in the ignition. I looked over at George. In that instant, I saw in my handsome, gray-haired husband, already deeply compromised by his brain disease, the seventeen-year-old boy with dark green eyes, home from college to take me on our first date. I was fifteen, in a brand-new white linen dress, my first pair of high heels, and a purse borrowed from my mother. A nervous and excited teenager, I glanced at his elegant profile as he put his hands on the steering wheel of his father's white Chevrolet and said to me, "So, where do you want to go for dinner?"

The wonder and promise of that long-ago night faded. I put my head down on the steering wheel and sobbed. George touched my arm and, momentarily, I believed he was trying to comfort me. I turned to look at him. "So, where are we going for dinner?" he said.

I started the car, drove out of the garage and into a prophetically sudden rainstorm. A new chapter had begun for both of us, in separate books still to be written.

~ ~ ~ ~

Many years ago, in my college geology course, our class was shown a sampling of the earth's core . . . layer upon layer, built up over the years, each a different color and texture, each containing historical markers of life and death in their embedded fossilized remains. So it is with me. I brought to this challenge all the layers of my life, all that I experienced, all that I inhaled and exhaled from those experiences. I came with old attitudes and beliefs, unfulfilled hopes and dreams, and my various ways of coping with life.

At the age of sixty-two, it was terrifying to suddenly find myself alone. At times, I thought I would surely die of the pain and loneliness. But I didn't . . . not because it wouldn't have been easy to give in to depression and despair . . . to say goodbye to life rather than stand up and fight for it. But I am a determined woman. I needed to know that I could make it on my own. That my life did not depend on another human being for its meaning or its duration. Life had dealt me some mighty blows over the years and I had survived them all. And though this one seemed more difficult to bear than any other, I knew that I was constitutionally incapable of doing anything else but going through and coming through.

The very moment my husband's dementia was diagnosed, everything in my life changed. Everything! Not one thing about the journey from that day forward has been easy. I went kicking and screaming into the night, to avoid the truth that despite my efforts to try to keep things as they were it was a ridiculous impossibility. Gradually, I realized that if I didn't figure out how to adapt to my life exactly as it was, I would die as surely as the man portrayed by Christopher Reeve in the movie *Somewhere in Time* died from his inability to remain in a former life no matter how desperately he tried.

But, how to do it? Where to begin? I was suddenly a displaced person, anxious, deeply depressed, my fears at an all-time high. Everything that had held me together—that I had identified as me, my, mine—had fallen away. I was running on empty.

As I worked with myself over the following weeks, months, and years I came to understand that from the ashes of my former life had come a profound gift. The tragedy of my life circumstance led to my own liberation. It stripped me naked. It made me look within myself to find the truth of who I really am, what I believe, and what I want for the rest of my life. Alone in my sixties, with more behind me than ahead, I felt like a prisoner facing the proverbial firing squad. To paraphrase Samuel Jonson: "It concentrated my mind . . . on me."

In my darkest moments in life, I wished for an older, wiser woman, a mentor with silver hair, kind eyes, and a face lined with experience. She would take my hand in hers and tell me she understood, had been there herself, and would help me get through whatever it was that had waylaid me. Little did I know that *I* would turn out to be that woman. When I went from being half of a couple to being alone, I gradually understood that I was the only one who could pull myself up and out of the carpet-licking lows and anxieties that came with the upheaval. I don't mean to imply that I did not have help along the way. Having psychotherapy, reading spiritual material and self-help books, and being with supportive family and friends are all to the good, and I experienced them all. But, when I closed the door on the outside world, I was alone with myself. And that is when my journey to the center of the bed really began.

When the door closed on life as I had known it, I had to sit still and be with the pain, fear, anxiety, depression, anger, and rage . . . be with the me I had brought to that day. I had to take myself apart and put myself together again. My adverse circumstances, it turned out, had created the perfect and, perhaps for me, the only climate for that process.

Moving to the Center of the Bed is a metaphor for moving to the center of my own life, to a place of independence and self-confidence, so that I could forge a new and meaningful life. It is about transforming myself from within, giving myself an inner makeover . . . more lasting than the makeovers I show up for at the cosmetics counters. It is about learning to become knowledgeable in all the ways I need to, in order to care for myself. That means dealing with practicalities, like finances and medical affairs. It also means finding my passion, the things that give me joy and fulfillment and doing them every day. And, in no small way, it means learning to honor the ups and downs of my emotional life, the terrible days, when no matter how hard I've tried or what I've learned about myself, getting out of bed seems an impossible act; and, equally important, not feeling guilty for the days that give me a profound sense of happiness in the midst of my grief.

As a conscious human being who wishes to grow in my life, I have to answer the deep questions with which life has presented me. And although sometimes it feels as if I'm floundering in the dark, that's where my deepest work is done. I have always searched for the light. What I have come to know is that *I* am the light.

Years ago I found this anonymous poem:

You cannot be given a life by someone else.
Of all the people you will know in a lifetime,
You are the only one you will never leave or lose.
To the questions of your life, you are the only answer.
To the problems of your life, you are the only solution.

I have tried every day since my husband left me in body and mind to live fully in the center of my bed. To weave the threads of my new life into a unique tapestry, a beautiful, significant, joyful, and satisfying life in a rediscovered self.

"*The most painful state of being is remembering the future,
particularly one you can never have.*"

S. KIERKEGAARD

Moving to the Center of the Bed

A Little Background Music

I grow up in an overprotective household, my parents in a constant state of fear and anger. My mother, a highly creative woman, is a perfectionist and hypercritical. I am threatened with abandonment for my childhood infractions and rebellions against too much control. I am rarely allowed to do anything on my own for fear that it will lead to personal harm, illness, or worse. Eventually I become an acquiescent child with a skewed sense of my self and my abilities and with a fear of life as well as death.

As I move into young adulthood my fears linger. The world is a frightening place, unfriendly and uncaring. And though fear is my constant companion, I force myself to do things in spite of it. But, I am never comfortable with me— just me. I never believe in myself, that I can handle whatever comes up—never trust my own decisions and because of that, I continue to fear being alone.

But I cover it up well. I become a super achiever with a supreme inferiority complex . . . and my fears about disease and death worsen. It is cancer on Monday, Leprosy on Tuesday,

TB on Wednesday . . . and on Thursday, when Mr. Wenker, my high school English teacher, assigns *Death Be Not Proud*, I am certain that book has landed on my desk to tell me that my recent headaches are from an undiagnosed brain tumor.

My father is more approving and loving to me. It is my mother's love and approval I seek, which never seems to manifest. But so anxious am I for it that I shape myself into the mold she has created for me. I am a dutiful daughter but with an arsenal of resentments buried deep. And when I leave for college, never again to live in my parents' home, I take from my volcanic home life a lot of misinformation about myself, about womanhood in general and about marriage. Mostly I carry within feelings of unworthiness, dependency, and fear. They are still with me when I marry in my last year of college and graduate with my husband's last name.

I am emotionally unready for the next part of my life or for much of what life offers me thereafter.

A Long Marriage, Briefly

I *am eleven years old and my future* husband is thirteen. We meet on a bus ride home from a youth organization picnic. He'd rather be with my best friend; but she has eyes for another. I try my best to console him. He's not interested.

We meet again on a blind date when I am fifteen. He doesn't remember the bus ride. I wonder if he'd still prefer my best friend. Over the next several years, we fall in love and marry when I am twenty and in my last year of college. He is in his third year of medical school (he entered college at the age of sixteen). I begin marriage a fearful bride, a know-nothing about the world.

Our marriage, like all marriages, is not uncomplicated. I try to be the perfect wife and mother that *Good Housekeeping* teaches me how to be. But there is an underlying anxiety and fear accompanying everything I do. I become a chameleon, taking on this idea or that way of doing things or saying whatever I think someone would like to hear. When I have my first taste of French food and bite into what is called a *pomme soufflé* . . . a tiny puff of potato with a delicate crust surrounding what seems to be simply . . . air, I finally have the perfect image of how I feel. I am all façade, living a false life, saying the right things, doing my job—but inside there is a feeling of nothingness. I live in my head, worrying, wondering, trying not to let my fears and insecurities take over my life

Regardless of what is happening inside me, I try my best as wife, mother of one, two, and then three. We bop from state to state . . . a few years here . . . ten years there . . . fifteen in another place . . . wherever there is an opportunity to fulfill more of my husband's professional goals. I want his success; but I never like any of the places we live. There isn't much I can do about it except to bloom where I am planted because I have a privileged life. But I never feel as if I am truly in a life that feels like my own. I don't feel like *me* but, then again, I still don't know who *me* is. I busy myself in the life I have with a man I love but who is also a very busy man.

From the beginning of our marriage, George's life is heavily committed to the demands of medicine and patient care. As he grows in his career so do his commitments as head of academic departments and professional organizations. Over the years, I am increasingly discontent about his escalating responsibilities, which take him too often away from home and family. I feel like a single parent in a two-parent home.

When I express my growing unhappiness to a few friends, their response is unsympathetic. "How can you complain? Your husband's a doctor!" Or, "You have enough money. You travel. You have everything."

I am embarrassed by my confession. Conventional thinking holds that a woman who has it all must be happy and fulfilled. How terrible for me to admit that what I have isn't enough . . . that the "good life" doesn't seem all that good . . . that something is missing. I am casting about for that something to ease the disquiet within me.

The belief that has inspired my friends' responses to my unhappiness . . . that having more means feeling less . . . that money or fame or power is enough to keep the demons from the door, is bogus. Neither material possessions nor the lifestyle they make possible prevents discontent. That is an inside job and only an inside job; and I have only just begun to know that.

In my embarrassment over the rejection of my unhappiness by my friends, I become more involved in my husband's career. Maybe, if I can understand the workings of all his committees and boards and what motivates his supreme dedication to them, we'll have more in common, and maybe then I'll be happier. I become super-organization wife . . . always present, by his side, well dressed, knowledgeable, seemingly interested, supportive. I even work for some of the projects he takes on. I spend countless evenings entertaining or at social gatherings that are extensions of his professional obligations. But, as he takes on more and more responsibility, I become super-dissatisfied wife.

As George and I begin to talk about the problems between us caused by his many commitments, professional troubles—the product of savage academic backbiting—begin for him, and in short order he is (we are) in the fight of and for his professional life. The fight takes two years. Incredulously, we lose. When it is over, my battered and bruised husband decides that he wants no more of academic life. He opts to finish out his career in private practice. We sell what we had believed to be our forever home and move to Florida, as foreign to me as the other places we've lived.

My husband and I are both physically and psychologically

exhausted from the years we fought the people who tried to bring him down and we make poor decisions because of it . . . to build another forever home and to open a private practice in ophthalmology in the worst of all medical climates as managed care makes its indelible mark.

When I close the door behind the builder, as he makes his last inspection of our new home, I lean against the door. All I can think is: *Why did we do this? I don't want this responsibility. I don't want this big house. I don't want Florida.* And, strangely, after all the years of fearing aloneness, what I suddenly want is to be alone. I know I am not the first woman who has ever wished to be alone, even within a privileged and loving marriage, but it will take me a long time to get over the guilt for the magical effects I feel those thoughts conjured.

The Knockdown Punch

Two years later, George's dementia is diagnosed. I wasn't in such hot emotional shape before; but I am unprepared for the feelings and emotions that come roaring at me after the diagnosis. When I have time to digest what has happened and to project all that it will mean for the rest of our lives, I find within me an explosive rage—a rage that has probably been building all my life.

I had been hoping to begin to sort out a life of my own choosing . . . a life that feels like my life. A life made up of things that *I* want to do, places *I* want to go, passions *I* want to pursue. I had given over most of my life to my husband and his work and I had hoped that a new beginning in Florida would awaken new possibilities for me. But now, I feel trapped. A horrible thing to feel, but even worse to admit. I know that the rest of my life will again be devoted to caring for the man I love, whom I've already lost, but caring in a way I've never imagined and for which I am not even remotely prepared.

Mass murder is politically incorrect. Instead, when I am

alone in the house, I choose a tennis racket and a pillow and smack it around until I am sweaty, yelling and screaming obscenities. I go to the local amusement park and hit softballs in a batting cage. I go swimming before sunrise and plunge to the bottom of the pool screaming until I am exhausted. Then I swim laps, punching and slapping the water and crying until my goggles are filled with my own burning tears. No one sees me. No one hears. Grief is solitary and anger is best expressed that way, too. I learned that lesson long ago.

After I vent my pent up rage, I start to think rationally. It's up to me now and I am terrified. I have so much to figure out and George is unable to help me in the ways I need help. I am worried about how much money we have and if it will be enough to see us through the rest of our lives without the income that George has always provided.

I did not take an active role in dealing with our finances throughout the years of our married life. From time to time I would ask George to make a little black book for me so I'd know what we have and what we owe in case something happened to him. But he never did. And I let it drop. Every once in a while I'd think about it and ask again. We weren't getting any younger and something could happen to him. But I continued to live like an ostrich—until the day life forced me to take my head out of the sand.

I contact our accountant and ask him to call our lawyer and investment counselor, ask them to review our files and set up a meeting with me as soon as possible. At that meeting I find out that my husband and I are living solely on our retirement funds. Because George was unable to become a part of many of the managed care insurance plans, he had to spend whatever income he received on his overhead and office personnel. We are in way over our heads. We have investments; but whether they will carry us through the years ahead will depend on how we choose to live. Most immediately, we must sell the newly built home in which we have invested all the money from our previous home plus most of our savings. In addition, I learn that there is a substantial loan for the purchase of George's office space.

Selling our new home is the third in a line of give-ups, giveaways, and paring down to essentials. Only a few years before I'd given up a home I loved in West Virginia and before that, one in Texas. They were difficult moves, but this one and the reason for it . . . is devastating.

In the next months, the fury with which I approach my new responsibilities doesn't give me much time to think about anything more than what is before me. I have to prepare our home for sale. I have to look for another place to live and to help our daughter Liz, who is George's office manager, close his office . . . but more heartbreaking for me . . . close the door on his distinguished medical career of forty years.

Disengaging

We lose a great deal of money on the sale of our home because we've only been in it two years and because of the large mortgage and loan payback. My anxiety heightens with the reality of the loss of money, but I am learning about the futility of hanging onto anything material thought to bring solvency. I cannot dwell on the loss because I have to continue to disengage, not only from a life we have only recently begun, but from a life and partnership of forty plus years, in order to move into the anxiety-provoking unknown.

After our home is sold, Liz, a single mother of our two grandchildren, suggests that I buy another house and that we all live in it together so that she can help me take care of her father. I do that . . . a lovely home . . . perfect for all of us. But, even with the best of intentions, it does not work. George is impatient with the noise of the children and he is beginning to leave the house unnoticed and wander too close to the busy highway nearby.

I have to sell that house after only a year and we lose more money. While the house is on the market, Liz and I search for separate places to live. George's behavior becomes more erratic and I more despondent. Living with his illness, the added responsibilities, and anxiety and deepening depression make it hard to get out of bed in the morning. I feel hopeless. When you have the flu, you know it will run its course and in a week or two you'll be back in the supermarket planning dinner. This time, there is no end in sight. There is no cure for George. There is no feeling better for me because every day I lose a little more of him.

I am beginning to be aware that soon my husband will require more help than I can give him. It is a terrible realization because I've believed all my life that family should take care of family. But, I must come to terms with the fact that I am neither physically nor emotionally able to give my husband the kind of care he will need.

As George's symptoms worsen, he enters an assisted living/dementia facility. It is a beautiful place I find after much searching . . . and a place he has visited with me and to which, astonishingly, he has asked to go. Since he saw the facility, he has asked me every day when we are going to live there. I have thought a great deal about moving there with him, so that I could watch over him. But I am not remotely ready for such a place. So, when he asks, I tell him that we have to wait a little longer. Finally, one day when he asks again, I say, "Well, honey, I am not ready to go there yet, but if you really want to go, you can." He says, "But I will miss you." I tell him that I will visit him several times a week and he says, "Then I want to go." This from a man who never wanted me out of his sight. Many people say to me, "Aren't you grateful that he *wants* to go?" I feel a lot of things; but at the moment, grateful isn't one of them. George and I will actually be separating.

11

The day I move him into the assisted living facility is the day I record in my heart as the worst day of my life. I place his furniture, hang up his clothes, and make his bed in a kind of stupor. George takes it all in stride. When it comes time for me to leave, I hug and kiss him. He is sitting on our bed that he wanted to take with him, fiddling with the remote control, trying to figure out how to turn on his television set, seemingly unaware that we are parting after forty-two years of marriage and will never again live together. I put my arms around his shoulders and kiss him again. He smiles and goes back to his remote.

I leave and cry the entire hour-long trip home, not truly believing what has just taken place, what has happened to our lives . . . that it is not a nightmare from which I will awaken, put my feet on the floor, and heave a great sigh of relief. I try to console myself with the fact that George is now in the right place for him. That the disease, true to the doctor's prediction, has taken away George's emotional connection and he isn't feeling lonely or unhappy. But that doesn't work. My sorrow is too great. Time is the great healer, so it's said. But I know that time will only bring both of us more misery. There is no way out. There is no pill to cure either of us. There is only life doing its thing—and at the moment, it really stinks. I've tried to be a good girl, good woman, best wife, friend, haven't I? I've worked on lowering my cholesterol. I've even been a den mother. I've gone through all the loss and anguish that has fallen to me in my life and I'm still here. And this is my reward? Where is fairness? Where is God, for God's sake? I HATE THIS. I HATE IT. I HATE IT!

The next day, Liz moves into her rental home with the children and I into the rental apartment I've chosen in the same complex George and I had lived in while we were building our home. The movers leave near midnight. When I close the door behind them, the silence is stunning. For the first time in my life I am really and truly . . . alone. I lie down on the unmade, newly purchased bed and cry myself to sleep.

Life Alone Begins

The life I wake up to on the first morning in the first place of my own is strange, frightening, and depressing. During the previous year, there was so much furious activity, so much business to attend to, that I was not remotely aware of what it would feel like to be surrounded by silence.

But, here it is. I am finally alone. Little old me in the center of the bed, in the center of my new life, hearing only the sound of my breath, the rhythm of my heartbeat. Mine is the only face in the mirror, my voice the only one I will hear, if I choose to speak. I get up to brush my teeth and look in the mirror to see . . . oh, God . . . my mother's face staring back at me . . . and my grandmother looking over her shoulder. I look older than I ever thought I could. I am immediately filled with fear and anxiety. I will be growing old alone. I am sobbing now and cannot stand to look at myself crying.

I go back to bed and lie very still. I listen to the birds, the sound of children laughing, a noisy lawn mower. Life is all around me. But I feel dead. A thousand thoughts pass through

my mind, none of them particularly good. A lot of "Oh my
Gods," "Uh-ohs," and "Oh nos!" And I realize that if I lie
there any longer I will not be able to get myself up. I go back
into the bathroom and run the bathwater and suddenly I am
aware of a commentator in my head: "You're taking your first
bath as a woman alone. And you're going to be eating your
first breakfast alone." Then she gets nasty. "Well, you once
asked for it . . . so, how do you like being a.l.o.n.e.?"

I've lost a great deal of weight from a diet of anxiety and
fear and have little appetite. But, I fix some toast and tea and
take it outside to the porch. Just the opening of the door to
the outside world is, symbolically and practically, wonderfully
healing. Opening to nature, even on the second floor of an
apartment complex, watching the exotic birds line up along
the small pond, takes my mind briefly off myself. Nature
knows nothing of human sorrow. It just is, and keeps on being
itself, reminding me that there is more to life than my own
problems. Looking outward, being in the bountiful beauty of
nature—even the strangeness of swampland—has always been
a linchpin for me. I breathe in the sweet morning air, already
drenched in Florida humidity, and decide to try not to think
of anything but eating my toast and drinking my tea.

But, what immediately comes to mind is Vermont.

I'd made small tries during my married life to do things
on my own. This may sound ridiculous to those who have
never been as afraid as I was to be alone. I'd always wanted
it, and at the same time was fearful of it. So, I'd fly to visit an
aging uncle in another state or my children at college. The
destination always brought me loving faces. I had never gone
away to be alone with no one to greet me or who cared that
I had come.

But, a year or so after we moved into our new Florida

home, I felt the need to get away by myself. George's behavior had changed. He seemed to be depressed and was emotionally distant. We talked about it; but he didn't think anything was different. As the days moved on, we talked less and less. Things between us were troubling. And then, two of our adult children moved back into our home, our daughter Liz, who was going through a divorce, with our two grandchildren; and our son, Bruce, who was in between careers. Our house was inordinately busy and I needed some time to myself to begin some new writing projects; but mostly to be away from all the activity just to think. I wanted to get out of the heat and back to the North and all the lush greenery. I looked on the Internet and found a small house to rent in Vermont. I was both excited and scared and chastised myself for being my age and still having so many fears about being alone. But I did it anyway. I flew to Burlington, rented a car, and drove through Montpelier to a little town called Calais.

It was gray and raining hard as I drove into the driveway. I carried my bags into the kitchen from the garage. The house was cold and unwelcoming and darkness was coming on quickly. Though this was the treasured home of a very kindly woman, my inner princess had a field day, as in: "I left my beautiful home for this??"

I turned on all the lights and chose a bedroom at the front of the house so I could hear noises if anyone approached. I put my suitcase on the bed, slumped down next to it and immediately let go of months of frustration and sadness and cried for a long time. Then I unpacked, took a hot bath, and read awhile in bed, finally turning off the light and shivering myself to sleep. One by one, my demons crept out of their caves. I awoke often and scared, in foreign territory, the night as black as any I'd ever seen, wondering who knew that a woman was in the house alone. Anyone who has ever spent a night in the Vermont outback knows how black and utterly silent it is. Murder plots unleashed themselves in my wild night imagination. I conjured the local morning newspaper headlines: "Woman Strangled by Stranger Hiding in the Bushes" or "Summer Tourist Raped and Sodomized by Vermont Vagrant." I got up and rechecked all the locks and peered out the windows into the opaque night. How would I ever make it through five weeks?

I didn't. I left after twelve days. Nothing was right. Including my writing. I had found a certain rhythm in my life there; but I had little contact with anyone unless I went into town to buy something. And I was less productive than I imagined I would be. For so long I had wanted something . . . someone to give me the life I wanted (although I wasn't sure what that was) . . . something . . . someone to make me happier, make me whole.

Vermont was not it. I was achingly lonely . . . but for what? Home? Where was home? I had a home . . . with a husband who was becoming more emotionally detached from me and returned children and grandchildren. Loving them all has nothing to do with it. Our home didn't feel like home anymore. But it didn't feel good to be out on a limb in Vermont either. My stay there seemed pointless . . . so I ended it with a sense of failure and shame.

Because my life continued to fall apart after I returned from Vermont, I didn't really see the value of what I'd done by going there, until this first morning of my new life, sitting on the porch of the small apartment I have chosen for myself. I no longer have the option of returning to a house where a husband and family live. But until this moment, I had not acknowledged the awareness that during my stay in Vermont

I had exorcised some of those old and ugly demons that had pursued me from childhood, and I had become unafraid of being solitary. I could sit in silence and read for hours without getting fidgety and turning on the television, or putting on a CD or running to the piano . . . or eating.

In short, in Vermont I had begun to be comfortable with *me*. I had started to build a foundation of experience I could trust . . . something that I did for myself . . . not related to any thing or any other one. In a rather profound way, I had been given a sampling of what was to come . . . as if it were somehow a test of my mettle—and I had passed.

The joy of that awareness is intense as I sit drinking my tea. I suddenly have great and tender feelings of compassion for that frightened woman roaming around that Vermont house searching for herself and for the same woman now sitting on the porch with her cup of tea. It is the first time I can ever remember having a compassionate or loving thought towards myself, and it gives me a kind of peace and comfort I have never experienced. I am alone with my self now and also with all the other mes that have come along for the ride. And, for the first time in my life, I am acutely aware that I feel safe and I know that I have a choice . . . to allow my overactive mind to continue to tell me I am afraid or to allow my heart to tell me I am not. I have stepped onto the path to begin a new journey and I can either sit down and let the moss grow over my toes or start walking.

I walk . . . back inside to the kitchen, wash my solitary dish and cup, and begin unpacking my new life.

"Fare Thee Well
For I Must Leave Thee"

I am unprepared for the suffering that is now a part of my days and nights and for how alone I feel in my suffering. Though I have a daughter living near me, I realize early on that I cannot, to be contemporary about it, download my personal files onto my child's computer. She is trying to deal with her own grief for a beloved father who is suddenly unavailable to her in all the ways she has known. And my son and youngest daughter are in different parts of the country, facing their personal loss and confusion.

I don't hide what I am feeling when we talk on the phone, but neither do I seek them out in my most difficult moments. As their mother, I am supposed to help *them* but they are hesitant to vent their grief to me for fear of making things harder on me. We are all keeping up appearances.

To add to the feeling of aloneness, being new to Florida I have no supportive community of friends around me. My dearest friends are scattered all over the country. But, what is the most hurtful is that so many people George and I had considered friends during his long career disappeared from our lives after his diagnosis.

My father used to sing a song while he was shaving:

"Fare thee well for I must leave thee,

Do not let the parting grieve thee,

And remember that the best of friends must part,
* must part,*

adieu, adieu, kind friends, adieu,

I can no longer stay with you, stay with you,

I'll hang my harp on a weeping willow tree,

And may the world go well with thee."

To me, it was simply a happy song sung by a man I loved with white cream all over his face.

But the words had prophetic significance.

George's professional life as physician, surgeon, teacher, and chairman of departments of ophthalmology, brought him into relationship with hundreds of colleagues. He was on boards and committees and once president of the most beloved of all his ophthalmologic organizations. And I was very much a part of his medical world. From the beginning of his training, we were a couple, a team. When our children were young and he had to travel to meetings, I could not go along. But later, as the children grew, I often went with him and developed many friendships with both his colleagues and their spouses. At those meetings, we women often had organized activities, or just joined each other to go to museums and lunches. We got to know a lot about each others' lives . . . our children, our accomplishments, our problems. I was a part of the journey of two of those friends who were diagnosed with breast cancer. In the evenings, we joined our husbands at elegant dinners. I knew, if not personally, then by name and face recognition, nearly everyone in the ballrooms and dining rooms that served our groups. George and I considered so many of them dear friends. But, they made me redefine the word.

When George was diagnosed with dementia it was as if the air around us had been tainted with a noxious substance that prevented approach. Less than a handful of those dear friends and colleagues have ever called or inquired about George's health or whereabouts, or to visit him, or to support me during the most terrible time of my life. Emotionally shattered and feeling more alone than I ever thought possible, I would give anything to hear the friendly, caring voices of those I had spent so many years getting to know and care about, not to mention to have their arms around me . . . but most definitely not a "How are you doing?" in an email. George and I had supported so many of them in their own troubled times, and now, when we are both in need, we are left on our own.

I am angry and incredibly sad about their lack of concern for us. And so I try *not* to think of them. But, in my worst moments, I do think about them and wonder how they could not understand how important it is in a life crisis to hear a comforting voice that simply says, "I'm so sorry. I care about you." Not to mention paying a visit with arms outstretched so that grief and fear can be expressed to someone lovingly familiar who holds and hears.

The good news is that, contrary to that old song of my father's, what I am learning is that the best of friends never part. When the world did not go well with me, I was lucky enough to have true friends and family who never left me. They have stayed connected, either in person or by the telephone, some daily, some weekly; but they are with me as I take each step on this difficult journey. I am continually grateful for their love and compassion. And so, I say my silent adieus to the others. If not forgiving, I am wiser for the experience.

Reality Check

*My old life is gone. I do a lot of why-*ning about it to myself. Why does my husband have to endure the ravages of dementia? And, in my worst moments, "George, you son of a bitch . . . Why did you get sick and leave me to fend for myself? This is not what I meant when I asked to be alone!!" I feel like I've been hit by a two-by-four . . . everything is distorted. My nerve endings feel raw and exposed.

As days come and go in my new little home, I am at first focused on the past. Because George and I met so young and stayed together, all my memories of important times include him. So, whenever I think back . . . other than to my childhood . . . and who wants to think of that? . . . George and I are together, hand-in-hand, laughing, embracing, traveling, wining, dining, blowing out birthday candles, playing tennis, carrying children. He was at my high school graduation and in the front row at my master's piano recital when I returned to graduate school at the age of forty-two, older than all my professors.

Most difficult of all are the snapshots that click into my head . . . snapshots of the little things that are the big things of my life. Like the times George, dressed so elegantly, was preparing his special coffee in our kitchen, and I'd come up behind him, put my arms around his waist and hold him close, inhaling his delicious cologne and feeling the strength of his body. Or sitting with him and watching his face as he listened to his favorite piece of music, Bach's *Chaconne in d minor*, played by Izzak Perlman, his eyes closed in a state of pure ecstasy. I feel like screaming, "No! Please, no. I don't want to remember." But I also don't want to forget. As George is gradually forgetting everything, I want to preserve every moment we've shared.

I also find myself missing old routines that spelled comfort for me . . . knowing how my days would be spent, what meals I would cook for my family, my morning piano practice, my writing schedule, picking up the phone to hear George's voice saying he loved me and did I want him to bring anything home for dinner. Those things that had given me stability compared to the anxiety I feel now.

But all the reminiscing doesn't do anything but keep the misery coming at full speed. I remember hearing Woody Allen say, when asked what he had learned from his trials and tribulations with his former wife (I paraphrase), that he learned about the ability of the human spirit to be distracted. So, I try to distract myself . . . cooking up a dish from a complicated recipe . . . writing until I am blotto, watching Turner Classic Movies with bowls of popcorn . . . drinking wine. But after the food and wine, the chapters written, the conclusion of the movie, I am still me with my thoughts . . . alone . . . and looking for something to make me feel not so.

Revving Myself Up

But *I am alone and there is no place to hide* and no one and no thing that gives me feelings of comfort for very long. I rage. I cry. I sit still and feel terrified. I sob my abandonment and loneliness. I look in the mirror and hate my wrinkling face and body. I torture myself with anxiety about getting old and sick.

The size of my grief bag is enormous because I am not only dealing with my present situation but also with a lifetime of losses and pain that I have never grieved. All my life, in order to survive, I protected myself from the emotional cost of grieving. But now, a precariously built protective dam has finally burst. It is the toughest and most turbulent time of my life.

On one of the many days blurred by their sameness, my loneliness is so acute I think I will die from it. I open the sliding glass doors and step onto the porch with a book in my hand. But it is too hot to sit outside and read and the buzz of the groundskeeper's lawn mower is annoying. I go back into the cool of my study and open the book. I cannot concentrate.

I try to write. Drivel . . . delete. I go into my bedroom and lay down on the bed and suddenly I am sobbing. I think I will never stop. But I do. I am still for quite some time and finally pull myself up and go into the bathroom and wash my face with cool water over and over again.

As I take the face towel from its ring, I look into my clothes closet. It is dark and quiet and I smile, remembering how I'd find my daughter Rachel in my closet when she was three years old, hanging onto my white rabbit fur coat (I can't believe I ever owned such a thing) and sucking her thumb. It suddenly seems like a good thing to do. No rabbit coat or thumb sucking for me, but I sit down under my clothes, breathing in the scent of my perfume, my arms over my knees, feeling the exhalations of the breath of life on my skin. It is a wonderfully comforting experience. Surrounded by the things that make up my everyday face to the world and the woman I have become I am suddenly overcome by a returning feeling of love for myself and compassion for the difficulty of my journey. It is a sweet, sweet moment and I feel peaceful and safe.

I am so tired of feeling terrible. I want to duplicate that feeling of sweetness and safety of sitting in my little closet in the larger spaces and places of my life. But how?

The next morning, as I lie in bed listening to the awakening birds . . . good, long sleep eludes me . . . I decide that this day will be a new beginning for me. And I will begin it by taking a sunrise walk on the beach. I love the ocean, one of the few things I do love about Florida. As soon as I make the commitment, that hopeful feeling returns. With a cheerleader's gusto I think, *I know I can do it. I can become the woman I've longed to become. I can learn to create my own happiness . . . my own fulfillment . . . a new purpose and meaning for a new life.*

Walking Myself Awake

T he transformation I am seeking literally begins on foot. I force myself outside of my protective walls and onto the streets as the sky begins to lighten, walking at a heart-stimulating pace, listening to my breath, feeling my aging knees and hips begin to loosen up. It feels so good to be out of the house . . . walking . . . alone.

Imagine that! I am hopeful and excited as I make my way along the concrete streets and finally through the sandy right-of-way to the beach. I breathe a sigh of utter contentment as I hear the waves breaking on the shore. I listen to the screech of sea birds, and say a silent prayer of gratitude: "*Thank you God for the breath of life . . . for the ears to hear these birds, the eyes to see the beauty of the sunrise, the strong heart that beats inside me, the legs and arms that propel me forward.*" It is the first time that I am truly able to get out of my own pain and into the world around me.

And I think . . . *I am still whole. I have a chance to begin again . . . from exactly where I am . . . my feet planted on the shore, my eyes on the horizon. Something good will come from what has happened. I will see to it. I am helpless to fix what has happened to George but I can fix me.*

I vow to remember this morning, this commitment I make to myself every day of my life.

After that morning I cannot wait for each day to begin so I can be out on the street, walking to the ocean, listening to my breathing, feeling my stride, paying attention to everything I see. The world looks brighter, the colors of the sky, the trees, and flowers more vibrant. After so many months of being unable to see beyond my own immediate problems I feel reconnected to the world around me.

One day, as I am moving along, I ask myself a question. Actually it is more in the form of wondering . . . "I wonder why". . . and I receive a swift and loud reply. I am startled . . . but not really. Because I quickly realize that I have reconnected with something that I have almost forgotten existed—my very talkative inner voices. Some people call those voices angels, some, higher consciousness, some even say it is God speaking through us. All I know is that from the day I first discovered them, years before this morning walk, the voices have guided me and provided me with a deep well of nourishing wisdom from which I draw sustenance. But for much too long a time I have been too preoccupied with my outer life to ask or to listen.

Suddenly being aware that they are still there for me excites me and gives me an incredible sense of comfort . . . of having found again the deepest, most precious part of me. It is a wondrous thing . . . like the proverbial jewel sewn into the hem of a beggar's garment. I know instinctively that what I have rediscovered is my ability to look at my life in a different way, from a different perspective . . . from within . . . from a deeper knowing than what my noisy mind provides.

The next day I walk to the beach, concentrating on those voices, asking questions, receiving answers, feeling as if a spiritual partner is guiding me. The questions come fast, and the answers faster. By the time I return home I am reeling with information, wanting to write it all down, but unable to retrieve much of it from memory. So, the next day I carry small cards and a pen with me. I'm sure I look strange to the people I pass, as I walk, stop, write, and walk some more.

When I get to the beach, I sit on the wooden entry steps and put down the cards, inhale the ocean's scent, watch the birds dipping and diving for food, sometimes closing my eyes and just listening. The feelings of peace are overwhelming. There is only this moment. I am in it and I have no troubles. It is just me, sitting on a step, watching the ocean, feeling the sun on my face. All is well.

Now, how can that be? Even with all that has happened . . . I am suddenly happy. I am alone, without my partner, and I am not afraid. I am just fine . . . more than fine. I am excited. I want to stand up and shout, "Hey, look at me. I'm OKAY! I'm really OKAY!!"

But, Am I?

*I*t is astounding that even with my life exactly as it is, I can still feel happiness. But I am also well aware that I have a lot of work to do on myself. Because I want that happiness to come from feeling fulfilled within myself. I want something that is not fleeting . . . but solid and lasting. I do not want to fear the future without George. I want to be confidently engaged in making a good one for myself.

And, in order to do that, I know I will have to find out how to transform years of self-doubt, fear, and anxiety into self-love and a knowingness that I am dependable . . . that I can count on me for everything. I have certainly been a mainstay in so many crises of family and friends. Now, I have to learn how to be there for me. No one is by my side any longer to do anything for me. Not bring me a cup of soup when I'm sick . . . not button that last button on my dress . . . not say thanks for the nice dinner . . . not hold me in the night.

I am going to have to open my trunkful of fears and

insecurities, pull them out, and look them in the eye. It is scary to contemplate, but I'll have to get unscared if I want to continue to move forward. And, I can only do that by facing anything and everything that has kept me from being the woman I want to be.

My Home, Beautiful Home

I start gently. I want to make my new little home beautiful. I have finished arranging furniture and putting into closets and cabinets those remains of my former life that I liked well enough to carry into my new life. I sit down in the middle of the living room floor and look around me. It isn't a pretty sight. Pink, pink, and more pink—the color of every third apartment in the complex. It doesn't go with any of the furniture I have brought with me. But, the apartments became condominiums shortly after I moved in and I had to buy mine or move out. I bought it and, now that I own the place, I can turn it into anything I like. I haven't been motivated to do much of anything, but I am suddenly excited and nervous.

Nervous because all the other homes I have lived in with George were "decorated" by others I thought knew more about style and color than I did. I had long ago taken in words that told me I didn't have good taste . . . in food . . . in clothing . . . in design. Those messages stayed with me and I never had enough confidence in myself to put together a lovely home on my own. But now, awakened daily to the reality of life alone, I know that I need to surround myself with myself—with what matters to me. To use the colors I love. To choose what goes on the floors and the walls . . . the texture of fabric, favorite photographs and paintings. I want beauty all around me. I want to wake up in the morning and go to sleep looking at something lovely, inspiring, something created by my own hand in a way that will give me a feeling of peace and well-being.

I get up from the floor and go into my study. On top of the computer sits my granddaughter, Carlee's, red Barbie doll shoe. I'd found the tiny shoe on the edge of the bathtub the day she moved out of our home with her mother and brother. It had made me so sad to see that little shoe and to know that I had to bear the loss of her small body in my arms every day so that her mother could begin to make a life of her own. I kept the shoe as a reminder of sweet times together.

Next to the red shoe is a baby sock with a Tasmanian devil on it that belonged to my grandson, Sammy, a tiny rubber chicken he gave me, and a rose that I dried from an inexpensive bouquet I bought myself when I was feeling lonely. There is also an African fertility god (out of commission) and a funny little key chain, both given to me by my son when he was in high school Next to my computer sits a mug with MOM written on the front. It was made by one of my children in grammar school and now holds my pens and pencils. On a shelf over the computer is a smooth, blue crystal egg I bought at a flea market in California and a small crystal bowl with a few white seashells I collected that morning of awakening at the beach. All of these things mean something special to me. And, if I want to make this home truly mine, I need to concentrate on surrounding myself with whatever I love.

I pick up a pad and pen from my desk and go back into the living room. In that small room there is already evidence of what is of supreme value to me. My piano stretches its 7' 2" frame across one wall, making it impossible to have anything more in the room than a single chair and an armoire. That beloved instrument has had, at different times of my life, a room of its own and even in my present circumstances it still has pride of place, despite the fact that company has to sit on the floor.

I go to it and run my hand over its black satiny top. I think about the loving trouble and worry it has always been to move that piano as George and I moved around the country. Witnessed, most recently, when I was treated to uninhibited bouts of cursing by the moving men as they hauled my fat baby up a flight of stairs to its second-story home, trying again and again to angle it into the small front door. Once in, they made me swear not to call them if I moved out.

I continue walking through each room, making notes, picturing the end result of a renewal that will give me a solid and soulful feeling of home. Money is a consideration, but I bought the condo at such a reasonable price that I can afford to spend a little more to make it mine. Over the next few months, I change the window treatments, carpet, tiles, kitchen and bathroom cabinets, appliances, and the paint. The colors I choose are a reflection of my present state of mind and mood, a calming neutral beige for the living/dining room, faux painted with accenting colors; a pale, restful yellow for my bedroom and bath; and for my study, wanting an energizing color, I choose raspberry.

After many weeks, when the remodeling and painting are done, I go into the storeroom and pull out of boxes photographs of some of the beautiful places I have been around the world and important events in my life. There is one of me with my piano professor just before I went onstage to play my master's recital . . . and a scroll, Dr. Shinichi Suzuki, the famous teacher of the Suzuki Method, gave me when I went to study with him in Japan. There is another photograph I took when we were invited into a nomad's tent in the desert when we lived in North Africa. It is of the nomad woman, wife, mother, on her side of the tent with the goats, making coffee for us, her foreign guests. I gather up personal photographs of family and friends and then some of the artwork George and I had collected that I love. Over the next few days, I sit on top of the piano, stand on a ladder, measure and hammer nails into the walls and place them all. My husband had always done the hanging. But I am teaching myself how to do it without making too many mistakes and ending up with holey walls.

I have several prideful moments as I walk around the apartment and survey my work. Even the bathrooms are places for art and whimsy . . . small paintings, a poster, a few shiny, black shopping bags from a perfume maker in Paris and one from the *QE 2* on which I had been privileged to sail. On the countertops, some African statues, one of which I drape with cherry amber beads I got at the same flea market where I bought the little egg. The seller of the beads blessed them with an African prayer.

The room I spend the most time thinking about and preparing is my bedroom, wanting it, needing it, to be a place of comfort and peace. Sleeping alone for the first time after having a partner at my side for forty-two years is a sad experience. My usual side of the bed to sleep on is the left, facing the bed. But, my new bedroom is so small that I cannot fit a night table on that side. So, I have to switch sides. That alone is strange. I am sleeping on George's side of the bed, even though it is a different bed. Everything is out of kilter. When I get up at night, I instinctively roll to the right to put my feet on the floor, and roll instead onto my Yorkie. It takes me some time to adjust to being on the wrong side. But, adjust I do . . . and then I decide I want to feel what it is like to sleep in the center of the bed. This totally confuses my little dog, who spends countless nights jumping back and forth over my middle-of-the-bed body.

And, for that distressed body of mine, I have lovingly chosen a mattress, pillows, a comforter, and the softest sheets I can afford. They make me feel cared for. And, when I make the bed in the morning, right down the center I put all shapes and textures of throw pillows . . . to remind me of my new place in the world.

The final touch is to fill my little home with green. I buy plants that can take the relentless heat and sun on the porch and put several inside the apartment that give it vitality.

Now, everywhere I look I see things that have special meaning for me and bring me pleasure . . . some double-edged with sadness. Sometimes there is no way to separate the two. But, everything turns out as beautifully as I had pictured it. I have trusted myself, trusted my taste and ability to make myself a home that reflects me. It has been a rare act of self-confidence.

I have lived in large homes with grand spaces, filled with the warmth and energy of a husband and three children. And, so suddenly, it seemed, one by one, the children left to make lives of their own. At the last, my husband left, too. And so it is here, in this little apartment that looks out into a treetop, that I have taken myself and where I am learning how to honor the silent breath of my own life. I am proud of myself for having the courage to confront one of my old bugaboos. I *have* created a lovely home. There it is, in front of me and all around me, a place of beauty, peace, and comfort.

I love it and love me for creating it.

This is a good beginning.

Chicken and Roast Potatoes for One

HOW TO EAT ALONE
by DANIEL HALPERN

While it's still light out
set the table for one:

A red linen tablecloth,
one white plate, a bowl
for the salad
and the proper silverware.

Take out a three-pound leg of lamb,
rub it with salt, pepper and cumin,
then push in two cloves
of garlic splinters.

Place it in a 325-degree oven
and set the timer for an hour.

Put freshly cut vegetables
into a pot with some herbs
and the crudest olive oil
you can find.

Heat on a low flame.

Clean the salad.

Be sure the dressing is made
with fresh dill, mustard
and the juice of hard lemons.

Open a bottle of good late-harvest zinfandel
and let it breathe on the table.

Pour yourself a glass
of cold California chardonnay
and go to your study and read.

As the story unfolds
you will smell the lamb
and the vegetables.

This is the best part of the evening:
the food cooking, the armchair,
the book and bright flavor
of the chilled wine.

When the timer goes off
toss the salad
and prepare the vegetables
and the lamb. Bring them out
to the table. Light the candles
and pour the red wine
into your glass.

Before you begin to eat,
raise your glass
in honor of yourself.

The company is the best you'll ever have.

This poem comes across the airwaves of National Public Radio one afternoon as I drive down one of the main boulevards in Jacksonville, on my way to have my car serviced. It resonates deeply within me and I think, *I have to own a copy of that.* More importantly, I need to own its message. Because it speaks the truth about honoring myself. A truth I have not always lived. Somehow, universal guidance brings that poem to me as I am wrestling with one of the most difficult things I have to do—eat alone.

I turn off the radio and muse about the fact that I haven't been to a restaurant alone since my working days at the United Nations—in my early twenties—when I'd spend most of my lunch hour shopping at Bloomingdales and then stop into Prexy's for a quick burger. I didn't like eating alone even then. I only did it because I was not allowed to eat at my desk. But eating out in Florida alone is something I absolutely won't do. Everyone will stare at me.

I remember reading an article in a woman's magazine about women dining alone. The author admonished women not to accept a table at the rear of the restaurant; but instead to ask for one up front where you could be seen and see everyone and everything going on. Also, no books or newspapers allowed. Just sit and eat and be a big girl about it. *Right!* But that message was for big girls. I am a fledgling.

So that leaves, for the moment, eating alone at home. Well, that should be a snap, right? I used to do it all the time . . . eat lunch over the sink while I prepared dinner for my family, or carry my sandwich around the house as I made sure it was clean and dusted for my piano students and their parents. But, this eating business, now that I am a.l.o.n.e. is in a whole different category.

I still love to cook, so I prepare good food for myself. But, it is a lot harder to set a place for me at my dining table and follow the directions in the poem than it is to fill my plate, turn on the TV, and watch whatever rolls across the screen. Because it blocks out the screaming silence. Electronic voices . . . laughter . . . noise is what I crave. I can't sit down at the table, face empty chairs, and think of all the meals I've cooked for my family and their lively chatter around the table. My husband telling me about his day, the kids eager to have their say.

The upside, perhaps, is that I can dine in my underwear or no clothes at all if that moves me. I can drop food in my lap, spill my wine, and who will see? But, it doesn't match the downside.

What is there about eating alone that feels so sad? I've always felt a tug at my heart seeing a man or woman dining alone in a restaurant. I never considered that maybe they were feeling fine about it. But even unseen . . . alone at home . . . I do not feel so fine about it.

It is one of the many things I have to learn to do. At first, when I sit down at the table, I find a running commentary in my head . . ."How sad that you have to eat alone now" . . . blah, blah! But, I stay with it and eventually I am rewarded. Something wonderful happens when I finally relax into myself and the food before me. No distractions. No television, no radio. Not even music, at first. Just me, the clink of my fork and knife against the china plate, cutting a crispy skinned breast of chicken, the taste of a perfectly roasted potato, the rich feeling of a smooth French Bordeaux on my tongue. I learn that I can enjoy the sensual experience of a fine dinner no less by myself than in the company of another. In fact, more so, without any conversation taking away my focus from the beautiful food I have lovingly prepared for myself.

I do some back patting, too. Because I am beginning to have more affection and compassion for myself and what I have to do now to honor the life I have. I am worth the effort it takes to care for myself in tender ways. Nourishing myself and enjoying my own good company are two of them.

Acceptance and Perception

*A*s hard as I try to have a positive and hopeful attitude as I learn to live alone, there are many days when I swim in an ocean of negativity. It is so hard to get used to the idea that I will live alone for the rest of my life. *This is not right. This is not where I thought I would be in my sixties. Whoever you are up there . . . take it back.* I close my eyes. *When I open them, let me be back in my old life. I'll be so much better at it. I'll be nicer, more understanding, more of everything good and less of what I wasn't so good at. Just give me the chance.*

I open my eyes and look around. Sometimes the answer is no!

I make a real effort to be less sullen, more upbeat. But it is a few simple things that actually help me to move into a different mood and mode of thinking.

One morning, as I am having breakfast on the porch, a memory of something that happened several years before surfaces. I was in California, at one of George's medical meetings. A friend who lived there took me to Green Gulch, a Zen Buddhist practice center in Sausalito, California, for a spiritual experience. After a meditation, a Buddhist nun told us a story on the subject of *perception*.

> One afternoon, after a rainstorm, a Buddhist nun walked out into the garden of her sanctuary. Everything glistened in the bright sunshine. Crystal droplets of water hung from the green leaves of the plants and trees. Everything was washed clean . . . renewed. She could smell the moist earth and the perfume of the abundant flowers. She breathed deeply and began her walk toward the far end of the garden. In the distance she saw something lying on the path. As the sunlight caught it, it glistened like a diamond. In the refraction of the light she saw colors of lavender, green, pink, and a bit of pale yellow. She marveled at the beauty of the object as she got closer and closer. In fact, she could not take her eyes from it. And suddenly there it was, at her feet. At last, she was able to see what it was that had so mesmerized her. It was a dog turd covered with raindrops.

A light goes on. I have a choice. Dog turd or diamond in the sun?

Not that I would ever describe my situation in either of those terms; but, I get the message.

Acceptance. This is what has happened in my life: illness has separated my husband and me. I have to move on without him.

Perception. How I choose to view what has happened dictates how I will respond to it.

As sad as George's illness is, it is also an opportunity for me to reexamine my life and myself and to move into a self-directed future. Life is challenging me once again, more than ever before, but I have a deep knowing within me that I am equal to it. The thought that I can perceive my life differently and use that perception to move out of a self-constructed tomb of gloom and into a perspective of anticipation and possibility is heartening.

To reconfirm, or perhaps add to my newfound sense that acceptance and perception are key to my moving forward, a few mornings after I remember the nun's story I wake up with a song in my head.

When I was a child and into my teen years I listened to Jimmy Durante, the Schnoz (the nose), as he was affectionately called. He was one of my favorite radio personalities, a singer and actor who later moved onto early television broadcasts and movies. A beloved figure to many of a certain age, Jimmy would sit down at the piano and play and sing. One of his favorites was: "Ya gotta start off each day with a song. Even when things go wrong." I haven't thought about that song for more years than I care to remember. But there is his gravelly voice in my head, belting out the tune, just for me. And I suddenly feel happy. I try desperately to remember the next lines of the song. After some time they come to me: "You'll feel better . . . you'll even look better . . . " I never heard the rest of the song because, at that point, Jimmy would always stop playing, stand up, and tell jokes. Then, he'd sit down and play more songs.

I lie on my bed wondering why that song this morning . . . but knowing without knowing that it is my inner wisdom at work. I had visited George the day before and when I came home I was feeling particularly sad. It was my sixty-fifth birthday. I told him and asked if he knew how old I was. In all our life together, George would never give a straight answer to a question. He'd always try to make a joke. It never was funny to me, but this time, when he responded by saying, "You're twenty-three," it was no joke. I was certain he really did not know. Later, as we sat together in his room watching television, he suddenly said to me, "Today is your birthday. You are sixty-five." And then he added, "Today is your final day." I told him I sincerely hoped not, but I knew that he was just reconfirming that it was my birthday and had lost the ability to express what he was thinking.

Later, George walked me to my car. We kissed each other and I drove out of the parking lot and watched him disappear in the rearview mirror. I cried all the way home, thinking about all the birthdays of our lives together, with so much fuss and fun. All the work I've been doing on accepting and changing my perception was challenged mightily as I made my way back to the ferry and to my life without him.

And, this morning, here comes Jimmy and his song. Reminding me.

I can see into the living room from my bed, and there stands my piano. I want to run over and start playing the song. I have wonderful neighbors who say they love it when I play, but I look at the clock. It's 5:00 a.m. I wonder how much they'd love me if I went in there and hammered out "Ya Gotta Start Off Each Day With A Song"? Maybe they don't want their day started with a song. So, I just lie there and ponder the affectionate way I have been awakened to a new day with the wisdom of Jimmy Durante, whose advice is no less pertinent and enlightening than that of any guru.

Today, I move a little further ahead. From that simple jingle has come a profound reminder. That it is all about acceptance and perception. That my life is this, here, today. But I have the power to change my perception of it. I can stay stuck in the muck of resistance and despair—or move forward. I can look at my life as hard luck, woe is me, or I can say, *I can handle this*. My choice is to keep looking at my own rear end or turn forward and steer myself into the next part of my life.

When sadness opens its eyes with me, as it seems to every morning, I often find myself in my old reality of fear and resistance. I have to summon every bit of courage I have within me and remind myself that my life is beautiful as it is and that each day I have an opportunity to do what I can to make it even more so. I must keep the promise to myself to remember the nun's story and dear old Jimmy.

Steel and the Grace of Creativity

uring the on-and-off periods of anxiety and fear I experience, I've been searching within myself to discover how I held myself together in times past when life overwhelmed me. What strengths did I have that shored me up and enabled me to move through those difficult times? And, could they help me now?

One of the things I discover is that I have a powerful will to survive. And my ability to survive what I am truly unprepared to handle emotionally is due, in no small way, to the fact that as a very young child I began building inside myself a core of steel, something indestructible that got me through. Something that did not allow me to fold up and die. I tapped against it throughout my life. Through all the deaths and traumas, I never gave in. In those crucial times, that steel core kept out devastating feelings and emotions so that I could act. I had people relying on me. I had children and a husband who needed my attention. When I was the one who needed attention the most.

Unfortunately, I learned too well how *not* to feel. Eventually, that steel core interfered with my life. It blocked out all the good feelings, as well as the difficult emotions, and I became numb to life. Now, in my quest for wholeness, I am learning that I can feel and also survive, even if sometimes it seems that the tears and anxiety and fear will never end.

I have also discovered that what helped me survive so many difficulties in my life is the grace of my own creativity. I have been given many gifts in my lifetime, but music and writing have been the balm that has salved my wounds and saved my life for almost all of my life.

When I was six years old, I was given a piano. I had begged and pleaded for one since the Sunday afternoon two years earlier when my mother's dearest friend sat me on the piano bench next to her as she played "Deep Purple" on her shiny, white, upright piano, her cherry-red fingernails clicking along the keys.

As that very young child, I had a different than customary use for that large instrument. When the anger and the shouting in my home got to be too uncomfortable, I'd close the door of the dining room, where my piano sat against the wall, and bang out whatever tiny tune was in my repertoire . . . and I mean bang. I'd also hit the keys with my shoe . . . not too creative . . . and hardly musical . . . but . . . anything to block out the sounds of my parents fighting with each other. Over the years, their warring abated little; but my skill at the keyboard increased and I was able to take myself away from what was going on around me by keeping my shoes on and finding appropriate music to express the deep emotions I could not openly express. I was actively using music as a support without really understanding what I was doing. But, it was most assuredly taking me through the crusty parts of my life.

My love for writing was at first, just as with the piano, a way to express what I could not say. Soon, the form it took became other than introspective journaling. I began to experiment with poetry, short stories, children's stories, a novel, newspaper articles . . . pages and pages every day . . . even writing stories for my piano students' recitals.

Writing and music are intertwined in their importance in my life. As life continues to happen, I cling to the two creative outlets where I find both catharsis and solace. On the occasions when things are too overwhelming to write about, I'll sit down at the piano. At other times, my grief takes the form of a poem or just pages and pages of rambling sorrow. The strangest times are when I'm at the piano and suddenly think of a story line and have to run to the computer to set down my ideas. Or writing a story and suddenly hearing a tune in my head and running to the piano to work out the song.

What I've also learned is that at times I can neither write nor play. When George was diagnosed with dementia, the very conjuring of the sounds of music made me crazy. Emotions were too deep. I did not play a note or write a word until months after I was living on my own. And then the sounds of my playing and the power of my own words became the floodgates of emotional release. It's a tricky thing. But I know which and I know when.

Sad to think of now, but for more years than I care to remember I devalued my own creative gifts. Measured against those of this super-talented friend or that star of the concert or literary world, I saw my own talents as only a way to hide from the exterior world. It wasn't until recently, when I began to think about the strengths and supports of my life, that I realized that the reason I feel so good when I am playing music or writing is because I am literally tapping into that great Source of sustenance. I am not hiding, but rather finding myself. When I am home alone, working on a piece of music or gazing at the computer screen, the little icon blinking at me, waiting for my words, I feel a rush of joy that is indescribable. I am quickly into another realm of reality, focused and flowing without an extraneous thought. I lose all sense of time and place and am relieved, temporarily, of the existential angst of feeling adrift in the great big Void.

If I stay connected to my work, I stay unafraid. Because I am connected to my self. My inner life is my real life. It feeds me constantly and renews me. I am finding that I can cope with whatever arises in my outer reality because my creative work provides me with my true center. When I go out, I often take a piece of my writing or a song I've written and fold it up to keep in my pocket. If I am in circumstances that may be anxiety provoking or may cause me to forget momentarily who I am, I reach for it and hold it in my hand. It is strength giving. And, I have realized for some time that, like mother's milk, what is used is quickly replenished. The Source of the creative flow is unending. I trust it as I have trusted nothing else in my life and I feel continuing gratitude for it and for the central role it plays in my life and well-being.

The Red Suit

I still find it strange to be living without responsibility to anyone and having no one responsible to me. I try to keep up old routines that are satisfying. My early mornings are spent swimming or walking and then writing. In the late afternoon I am shopping for food or in a bookstore or practicing. I cook dinner for myself. Sometimes I spend evenings with my daughter and grandchildren. I watch television. I listen to music. I read a lot. I am, mostly, solitary.

This morning, after my bath, I stand in my closet trying to find something comfortable to wear for a day of writing. As I pull a pair of slacks from its hanger, I see that something has fallen to the floor. It's a beautiful red suit, one of the pieces of day and evening clothing I wore in my former life of travel and grand occasions. I brought all those clothes with me into this new life of mine. I put the suit back on its hanger and slowly sort through the rest of the colorful, elegant pieces at the back of my closet. Some still have price tags attached. Then I look at the things I wear every day to sit at my computer or on my piano bench.

Lately I have been buying clothes that give me comfort . . . like a too-large cardigan sweater of soft cotton, a jacket that feels like my childhood flannel pajamas, stretchy tops. Nothing that constricts. Only those things that allow freedom of movement and that feel good next to my skin. And most certainly, nothing dressy. So what I am trying to choose from are slacks . . . black, beige, white, jeans, tee shirts, sweaters, tennis shoes, sandals. Quite a contrast to the things I wore in "my other life."

I haven't dressed up in a very long time. I've met a few single women and occasionally we go out to dinner at local restaurants where casual means anything goes. And I don't see on my horizon, at the moment, parties and fancy affairs where I'll be able to wear any of those beautiful outfits hanging there. I have promised myself many times that I will give them all away. I certainly have had time to do it. But, they're still here . . . because I've dreaded it. All those beautiful dresses, their threads woven with so many memories. I should have put a blindfold on and tossed them all in a giveaway bag. But I didn't and I won't do that now. Today, I'm finally going to tough it out . . . eyes open. More things to let go of . . . if I can.

I dress and put on my makeup. Once breakfasted, I go back to my closet. I take out the clothes that I wore . . . my God . . . was it only a few years ago? I lay them all on the bed . . . dresses, suits, evening skirts and sweaters, blouses, shoes, purses, jewelry. I open the armoire in the living room to its mirrored inner doors, pick up the dress on top of the pile on the bed . . . long, black velvet with a partially plunging neckline and spaghetti straps . . . and stand before the mirror looking at myself . . . remembering.

I hear dance music. I see myself with George, my cheek

pressed against his . . . his silly old-fashioned dips that make me slip and nearly fall, pulling him down with me before he rights both of us. And I see the two of us laughing. I catch the look of my face in the mirror. I am smiling. And then I am crying and then sobbing. I take the dress back into my closet. I cannot let go of this one. I hang it up and stand there, huddled with the dress and the memories.

I hear children's voices. I move to the bedroom window and raise the shade. Two little boys are squirting each other with water guns, aiming, hitting their targets, and squealing with delight. What would it feel like to experience such fun . . . such spontaneous joy again? The boys run off the grass and onto the concrete path leading to the pool. The mother in me looks to see if there is an adult in attendance. A woman across the way, where the boys were playing, runs out of her porch, the screen door slamming behind her, yelling at the boys to stop. I let down the shade.

I take in a deep breath. Back to it.

Now I have in front of me a black-sequined suit with a too tight, short skirt . . . the one I wore to dinner at Commander's Palace in New Orleans and could hardly sit down . . . how those sequins annoyed my bottom! I lift the jacket to my nose. Do I sniff Cajun spices . . . crawfish etoufée? I close my eyes. I will never get through this. I take the black suit into the living room and lay it on the chair. Back to my bed. Next . . . a multicolored shirt dress. I'll never wear it again . . . didn't really like it when I bought it . . . nor this green one . . . shoulder pads too big. Next, purple and emerald silk . . . the one George's dearest friend, Hank, loved so much. He'd run his hand up and down my back, feeling the silk, muttering sweet nothings . . . all in fun. He died suddenly at the airport the day after I wore that dress. Onto the living room chair with all of those. Another few pieces . . . a long purple skirt and gorgeous white organza blouse . . . oh, how I love these . . . I have to keep them.

Next . . . the red suit. I find the box with the matching red satin shoes with the special jeweled ruby clips. I take them out, slip them on, and go back to the mirror, holding the suit up to my neck and pressing it into my body. George loved this suit . . . said it made me look like an hourglass. I put it back in my closet. Next . . . next . . . next.

I end up with only four dresses to give away. I put them in a garment bag and leave them in the living room. The rest are keepers . . . the purses, too . . . and, of course, the matching shoes and jewelry. I put them all back in their places in my closet. I'll wear them again.

I sit down on the bed, suddenly so weary.

The worlds of fantasy and reality collide.

I'll wear them again? Where? Maybe the cute delivery guy will invite me to the UPS wingding. Maybe my fairy godmother will arrange a ball in my honor. Maybe some old friend will remember I'm alive and take me dancing.

Maybe not.

Why am I hanging onto those clothes? They are my past. They are out of date. I don't need them to remember the good times with George. The memories are in my heart. What I need are some new clothes for a new life.

I go back into the closet and take out the old dresses, the purses, and the shoes and lay them on the bed. This time, I put them all into bags and boxes. The fabulous faux gems I've collected over the years I put aside for my grandchildren and their friends for Halloween.

I keep only three dresses . . . three dresses I will never give away or wear again. My three piano recital dresses. One . . .

long, pale-rose, with sequins and pearls on the sleeves, has in its folds the remembrance of my youngest child, confiding to me as she came onstage to present me with flowers, that as I played, the light caught the sequins and made them sparkle like fireflies. The second dress, pale pink and gauzy with a satin ribbon around the waist I wore at my Master's recital. It always made me think of old-fashioned lawn parties with large-hatted women having lemonade and sandwiches. The third is from a two-piano recital, at which my piano partner and I premiered a contemporary composer's work. He was in the audience. The dress for the occasion . . . maroon velvet with cream-colored lace lapels. When I look at those dresses, and I do often . . . especially when I am low . . . I am electrified. I am happy and proud . . . proud of the woman who worked so hard to make it to the stage . . . who hated playing in public but fought the fear and did it anyway . . . and who lived to love herself for it . . . and to love her playing.

Suddenly, I am crying again. I am looking at the recital dresses but I am really looking at myself and the strength and power of the woman I was. And I know with certainty that I am going to make it because I am that same woman . . . today . . . standing in my closet with no less courage and ability to face my fears and to move through them. I embrace myself and stand for a long time in the quiet of that awareness.

I make several trips down to my car and load the giveaways into the trunk. I will find a good home for them all. I come back up to the apartment. It feels cooler . . . the air lighter. I go back to my closet. Lots of empty hangers. I expect to feel a great sadness. But, surprisingly I do not. I feel relief. The cleared out closet has cleared my head. Today is the day for letting go. A little bit at a time, I am able to say goodbye to what no longer serves me and to deal with the reality of now.

Progress.

Baby Fat

The other day I read of a dying woman who turned away the baked potato on the hospital lunch tray. She didn't want to look fat when she died.

As strange and sad as that sounds, I actually understood her most likely lifelong imprisonment in a woman's food/fat dilemma. It set me to thinking hard about my own problem with food and my negative attitude towards my body. Because no matter what I've tried in the past, these have hung on like the boyfriend who never quite got the message that I didn't want him around anymore. And so, since I've decided to work on myself and try to let go of whatever has been keeping me from becoming the woman of my dreams I might as well have a go at this. Maybe this time I can do it.

No small part of my life has been spent hating my body. It started when I was young and fat . . . *baby fat* they called it. Every woman in my family was overweight, but *my* fat seemed to be the object of everyone's concern. My mother was a great cook. And her mother, who was about 5' 1" and weighed over 200 pounds, was a fabulous cook and seamstress. She used to make me special dishes when I visited. And special dresses as well.

When she came to our home in New Jersey for a visit, she'd take my measurements and go home to New York City and create my dress. She'd come back a month later and try it on me. I still remember the *tch tchs* as I stood there, taller and wider than the month before. She would have to let out seams, let down the hem . . . redo. I wandered off after the fittings, burning with shame and hating myself and my *avoir du poids*. No one mentioned that a month between fittings may have been too much for a growing female body. But, I had already gotten the message. Nothing normal about that. It was not acceptable for me to gain weight.

When I was a chubby twelve-year-old, I went off to summer camp and found an opportunity. I hated the food. That fact, plus eight weeks of constant physical activity, melted the baby fat away. I wasn't thin; but I was on the way. And, I had a taste of the admiring looks and words my parents heaped on me. That was also about the time my relatives began dying off. Heart disease took my grandmother first and the rest followed suit. Overweight, sedentary smokers almost all . . . but I didn't consider the cigarettes, or the lack of exercise, or all the stress of their lives, or the possibility of underlying physiological causes. No. I only focused on the fat. I equated it with death and from that time forward, fat on me was equal to a sentence of early demise.

I never again was fat . . . but I had begun a lifelong complex called, I found out much later, *body dysmorphia*. I was hypercritical of my body, particularly my hips, my stomach, and my thighs. My self-critiques didn't jibe with how others saw me; but I was obsessed with not gaining weight. I was never anorexic or bulimic. I don't know why not, because I had such an intense fixation about controlling what I ate. I also was never underweight or thin until later, when I developed stomach problems. But, I always watched what I put in my mouth and hated myself if I overindulged. A few pounds of weight added and my mirror screamed back, "You are obese." And yet, strangely, I loved people who would most likely be considered greatly overweight in our society. Loved to hug them. Loved to watch their personal indulgences, loved the smoothness of their skin. Loved them the way I loved my grandmother for her sweetness and love of me, despite her *tch tchs*. But fat on myself . . . no! No!

From those early days, I never remember being free of thinking about what I was eating and the harm "bad" (delicious) food might do to me. My life was spent denying myself so many pleasures of the table. Because if I succumbed to temptation I would be FAT and then . . . die. Part of my fear of fat was a clear fear of being like "them," identifying with all the family members whose lives were cut short by food . . . or so I thought. So, if I did everything they had not done, I would have a different future. In fact, that's what happened. I developed a healthy lifestyle but . . . big but . . . I went to the opposite extreme.

I remember an aunt of mine, not known for her warmth or tact, saying to me several years after my wedding, "Oh, you're still thin. I thought you'd let yourself go after you got married." Other than the confusion I felt from the backhanded compliment, I remember pondering those words . . . "let yourself go." It had a nice ring to it. "Let yourself go" . . . yes . . . stop hanging onto all that neurotic behavior. What would it feel like . . . to let myself go . . . eat what I wanted . . . wear a dress with an expandable waist and push it to its limits? It made me at once happy and terrified. Of course, I never did let myself go. I also didn't realize that there was something between self-indulgence and self-denial . . . *moderation.*

But, at this late hour, can I really develop a new attitude about my body, food, and health? Is there some way that I can eat, even indulge in some fat-filled fun foods, and not feel as if I'll have to pay off the Goddess of the Waistband? Or test cholesterol levels monthly? Why not a rich and creamy ice cream cone without a topping of guilt? I've been on every popular quick-fix diet since I was a teen, starting with bringing hard-boiled eggs and celery in my lunch bag so I could fit into my high school prom dress. Then, there was the grapefruit diet, the Scarsdale diet, Pritikin, the raw foods diet, rice cakes, high protein, low protein, no protein. If it tasted like tree bark, it must be healthful and I tried it. I "beaned" myself into oblivion . . . black ones, garbanzos, kidneys, pintos . . . greatly adding to the country's gas reserves . . . high carb, low carb . . . no carb. I mistreated my poor body for years and paid for it later with a rebellious stomach. But . . . I wasn't fat.

What crazy ideal do I still have in my head? I had a husband who loved me, loved the way I looked, thought my naked body was beautiful. My children thought I looked great. Friends, too. Why don't I? I go way back in time to hear my grandmother's *tch tchs* . . . my overweight mother's criticisms, the taunts of young classmates. How sad it was and how sorry I feel that I had to endure such things.

Okay then. Enough! No more dieting . . . ever. Only healthy eating . . . and indulgences when I want them. This pronouncement strikes fear in my heart. It is scary to think about giving up past behavior, even though I'd fare better without it. But, I am really ready for this one. I am also worried . . . because I am alone with myself and maybe if I ever get over this fear of food and fat I might stock my favorite ice cream, bags of Milky Ways, Ho Hos, peanut butter cups, and . . . whatever. What if I have a really lonely evening and eat the whole container of Chubby Hubby? Well then . . . if I'm really over the fear, I won't care . . . I'll just enjoy it. Okayyyy!

What I decide to do is give myself a project. It makes me salivate just thinking about it. I decide to make a list of all the foods I have ever loved, including foods that I've eaten on trips to France with my husband. I don't get too far before I start daydreaming about those trips and the food. George and I traveled to every part of that beautiful country, wandering cities, countryside, vineyards . . . loving the history, the architecture, the museums. But our trips were truly centered on the table . . . three-star dining . . . the best of the best cuisine and wine a person could ever be privileged to take in. Heaven on a Limoges plate. Nirvana in a crystal goblet.

I picture myself in France, at table, so happy, so filled with rich and delicious food . . . butters, creams, sauces. Not concerned with gaining weight . . . just grateful for the pleasures the chef created. I remember my happiness talking to some of those great chefs about the relationship the French have with food. I remember watching the other diners at table . . . particularly the women. None were fat. All ate with gusto, sitting at table for hours as one course followed another. Plates were cleaned. Lunch was a delicious three hours long. And I joined right in. Over there, I became one of them . . . relishing the perfection of the table, the way the food made me feel . . . so connected to my sense of well-being, my body thanking me. I didn't care if I died on the spot. I wanted my last meal to be *quenelles de brochet* . . . a kind of seafood dumpling in a rich lobster cream sauce . . . and not chopped tomatoes and nonfat cottage cheese.

Sitting in my study, I crave the taste and the feeling of the love that went into cooking that fine French food. And in the moment, I get it. I really get it. That woman who dined with my husband all over France is the real me. A liver and lover of life and food. Not the fear-of-fat driven little girl/teen/woman/ mother/grandmother.

With that revelation, I begin a return to my true self . . . the one who loves to cook and eat with abandon.

I have the desire to run out and buy some groceries so that I can make myself a rich, comfort food kind of meal. Instead of denying the urge, I do it. And while I am in the supermarket, I have another idea . . . something to jump-start my plan to have a new relationship with food and with my body. I quickly finish my shopping and drive home.

I decide to create a ritual, a symbolic tool to help end my negative thinking, behavior, and the suffering it has brought me. Something visual that I can re-image again and again if I am tempted to move back to a former mode of thinking. I decide to burn all my diet books. There they stand, on the shelves next to my revered volumes of Julia Child, Jacques Pépin, James Beard, and Lidia Bastianich. One by one, I lift the diet books out and take them over to the fireplace. I sit and look at them all stacked up and shake my head at their numbers and variations. And then I have another idea. I need reinforcements!

I go to the computer and send emails to my closest friends who are all aware of my fear/love of food. I tell them what I am going to do and decide on the exact time of the bonfire . . . 6:00 P.M. Eastern Standard Time. I ask them to send me their good vibes at that time and to raise a glass to my new awareness. It is now 3:00 P.M. I go back into the living room and sit down next to the books and begin tearing them up. I can't express how freeing it feels to be ripping the guts out of those books. My little dog, Pooh, who thinks that when I am on the floor it's playtime, runs over with his rubber duckie for me to throw around for him to run and fetch. I tear the books, throw the pages into the fireplace, tear some more, throw the rubber duckie, more than once getting confused and throwing the rubber duck into the fireplace. Fortunately, no fire yet. When I am done, I look at the spines of the books lying on the floor, useless. I am gleeful. A lot of people have made a lot of money on me and my fear of food. But no longer. I dump them in the trash and get out pots and pans to prepare my favorite dinner. Fried chicken, warm potato salad, and mayonnaise-rich coleslaw. From time to time, I go to the computer and am happy to see that every friend I have written to has responded that they will be symbolically with me at my bonfire. All is set.

A little before 6:00 P.M., I pour a glass of wine and grab a piece of paper and take them with me into the living room. I write the following and then raise my glass to myself and read my words aloud:

"I am burning my fear of food, my attachment to past behavior, my negative thinking about my body, a belief system that has never served me, an artificial ideal that can never be achieved. I am thankful for my body, full of health and vitality, and I will nourish it with delicious food. I thank my friends who support me with their love and understanding tonight. May what I do now always serve to remind me who I truly am and what I truly believe . . . and that life is to savor . . . with good food and drink."

I take a sip of wine, put the glass down, and strike the match. The diet book bonfire is lit. What a beautiful sight. It takes an amazingly short time for all those pages to be consumed. I think about all the years of torment spent poring over those books—and they were gone in minutes. I feel wonderful. And . . . the ritual has whetted my appetite. I take my scrumptious dinner and glass of wine out to the porch and enjoy my own cooking as never before.

As the days move on, I stay vigilant lest the old beliefs and behaviors about my body image and "killer" food rear up and take hold. It isn't easy to change what has been imbedded lifelong. But, I am more and more successful in developing my own attitude about what I eat and enjoying it in a way that I never believed I could. And, too, I try to remember daily to love this wonderful body of mine that moves and breathes and wants to be fed deeeelicious food.

At the end, I plan to eat the potato!

"Who do you think you are, anyway?"

All of my life I have unconsciously taken as truth the sometimes harsh critical things I'd been told or inferred about myself and my abilities or lack thereof. I learned that the world was a dangerous place . . . fearsome and unfriendly. And that I was unequipped for taking it on. Those unexamined, long-held beliefs kept me anxious and fearful. I could never truly embrace life. I was afraid to take chances, afraid of the next challenging event that might catapult me further into panic and anxiety. Not that it appeared so outwardly. I developed a persona that was directly opposite to what I was feeling inside. But now, it's really time to put the inside out there and to answer the question I was asked so many times in my youth: "Who do you think you are, anyway?"

Indeed. Who am I? What do I know as truth about myself?

I am complex. Like most people. I know enough to know that I will never really understand everything about me that I'd like to. But maybe I will learn enough to be able to bring more awareness to my new life situation and the decisions I have to make every day. And that can only happen if I make them from a mind and heart that are my own. From a point of view that is my own. I am responsible for everything I think, everything I say, and everything I do. And so, I want to make certain that those self-numbing epithets I've lived with up until now are reinterpreted in my own words.

What I am doing is taking down from my shelves all the unauthorized personal biographies . . . those volumes of mythology written long ago by the very people entrusted with caring for my heart and soul . . . and which I've kept in my library over the years. Books with venomous titles that infected every part of my life, such as *Sheila is Always in a Fog, Sheila Doesn't Live up To Her Potential, Sheila Is a Hypochondriac,* and *Sheila Hasn't the Slightest Clue About Money.* There were lots more. Poor Sheila! But, I'm still here. And it's time to write my own books, figuratively and literally. Time to dedicate myself to understanding and changing the myths and replace them with what I know from my personal experience to be the truth.

I'm going to tackle a big one today. In fact, I could write a separate book on this one because it's been one of the most difficult to challenge and reframe. It was carved deeply into my being. *Sheila is a Hypochondriac.* This one has its roots in my childhood . . . times in which I had little control over anything. Times during which I developed a lifelong fear of illness . . . mine, mostly. Now that I'm older and without a partner, learning to handle as much as I can alone, I have to find the truths in all the fear and anxiety.

It's really difficult to believe that I still hear old voices from my childhood . . . voices that threatened abandonment. *"No one will take care of you if you get sick"* or *"If you get sick again,*

I'm going to take you to the hospital." Threats that usually followed my refusal to wear my boots or raincoat. I guess my parents didn't know about germs causing sickness. Or maybe they did, but their threats were effective tools to keep me in line with their wishes.

My parents didn't agree on much; but they were both deathly afraid of death, particularly mine. It was a dangerous time for children in the late 1930s and '40s when I was growing up . . . before the polio vaccine and a lot of other miracle drugs and surgical procedures that now save lives that were once doomed. But, parental admonitions rather than illness were more responsible for nearly scaring me to death. However, I didn't die and I guess that was their point.

But I did get sick.

Apparently I had many bouts of bronchitis, or croup as they called it. No one gave a thought to the fact that a houseful of cigarette smoke might endanger young lungs. My parents had their own cure . . . the croup tent. The tent was more objectionable and frightening to me than the disease. It burned itself into my memory and became a subject I returned to again and again in my thinking and writing. The croup tent was created by draping sheets over the four posters of my bed. A hot-air vaporizer was put under the tent and I sweated out the chest congestion for as long as it took. It was a sad and lonely time for me . . . lying under those moist sheets, wondering if I was going to be abandoned or die because I'd gotten sick yet again.

This fear has no quick fix. I've confronted it before . . . but not with as much determination as I have now. I am ashamed that in my sixties I am still under the influence of old controlling threats that caused my tender child's heart to shake. But, it's time to get real. I am not that child anymore. In fact, I think back to when my own children were young and we all came down with the flu together and my husband was spending days and nights at the hospital. I had to care for all of us, feed, water, diaper, medicate, and sometimes sleep in my babies' cribs with them. A difficult time . . . but we all survived. And more recently, several months ago, I experienced being sick alone for the first time. I had a fever, took my dog out, drove to the doctor's office, and then to the local pharmacy, and made and fed myself chicken soup.

The truth is that I am more than equipped to take care of myself—and what's more—I will never abandon me. If and when I need help, I can find it in my physicians, my family, friends, and even kind neighbors.

One myth tackled. Tomorrow and in the days that follow I will try another and another until I am satisfied that I have rewritten all the negative titles to suit my authentic self.

From Woo Woo to Jung

*I*n *my search for a spiritual home and for* ways to understand my self and the human condition, I do a lot of investigating. I read many self-help books, books on philosophy, religion, psychology, books promising enlightenment if only I'd try this diet, breathe this way, sit in this position. I try Chinese herbs, acupuncture, acupressure. I read books about goddesses, crystals, angels, fairies, Zen Buddhism, Tibetan Buddhism, about JuBus (Jewish Buddhists.) I read much about the soul. I read much about our Native American culture. I read books based on the idea that philosophy can replace antidepressants. I read books written by a medium that inspires me to consult him . . . a visit that is heart-pounding and life-changing. I read about psychics and consult one from time to time. I visit people who claim to channel guides from beyond. I purchase Tarot cards and Runes. I learn different forms of meditation. I read about mystics and Yogis and Shamans. I read books on staying in the Now and books on what comes later. I sit in churches and try synagogue again. I am open to exploring many things, some of which are a little *woo woo*. And, at last, I end up in the lap of Carl Jung, introduced to me by my gentle and wise therapist, Barbara. His work, along with that of Joseph Campbell and Jungian analyst James Hollis become a primary source of wisdom, nourishment, and solace for me, helping the unknown that is myself through many a dark night.

Every book gives me something to take away . . . sometimes only the awareness that it holds no value for me. But I know now that I cannot read myself to heaven. And that I am my own best guide toward a life of spiritual meaning.

And so, on this day, I am feeling the need to let go of those books that are no longer of consequence in my life. I pile all of them on the floor and for the rest of the afternoon I sit, turn pages, and turn back time. I am witness to the beginning of my quest, what I've explored and moved through and . . . where I am at present. It is interesting and revealing. Some books with dog-eared pages, underlined, highlighted in yellow or pink, notes written in the margins with exclamation points or question marks or "Yes!" or "Ridiculous!" or "Who says so??" Some books still marked at a page to which I obviously intended to return, but the rest of the book looks unread.

At the end of the afternoon, I have filled several cartons to give away. I replace on my shelves, with great nostalgia, the first books I read that opened me to a different way of thinking and being in the world. I keep the Runes. They are strange and wise and fun. And I keep the works of Jung and Hollis and Campbell.

I will most likely buy more books that interest me in the spiritual or philosophical or psychological realms. But never again with the idea that they will answer my questions. What I know more and more every day is that the answers are within my self. And I still have much to explore.

The Medical Maze and Haze

I have had a life with a doctor husband. Someone who knew the system, knew the best colleagues to recommend for whatever ailed my children and me. Whenever I paid a visit to one of them and opened the door to leave, there was George, waiting, in his white coat, calming, reassuring. He halved my worries. I relied on him. I had his hand to hold. I went home to him.

And then, he was gone.

I try to avoid doctors now. When I see white coats I cry for all those years of seeing George in his own white coat . . . when he was first in training and when he chaired departments. I cry for the times I'd visit him in the clinic, see his handsome, smiling face. Hear him talking so kindly to his patients.

But I cannot always avoid. I try on doctors like I try on dresses. It is tiring. I revere the medical profession that was so dear to my husband, but not always the men and women who practice it, too often brusque and insensitive. And now I sit with myself in sterile offices, conjuring old fears. No one waits outside the door to hug and reassure me. Aging alone is hard.

Getting sick alone is harder. Projecting how sick I may get is the worst . . . the anxious moments not knowing if something is wrong . . . and if it is, will it be a BIG thing . . . waiting for the radiologist to read the mammogram and say I'm fine . . . but what if she doesn't?

I will walk home alone no matter what happens. That is just how it is now. I have to carry the burden of my own fears and the responsibility for my own care. I know that. But some days, on top of all the other things that are now my responsibility, I want to say, "Please, somebody . . . be with me . . . hold my hand. Tell me I don't have anything to worry about. Kiss my cheek and take me home."

Mea Culpa

*If I can ever find my elusive birth certi-*ficate I am certain that I will find stamped on it in capital letters my real middle name: GUILT.

I have nothing but time to think now, and I find that some days I am flayed with feelings of inordinate guilt: If I hadn't once wished to be alone, I wouldn't have magically conjured George's illness. Nor would I be experiencing such indescribable grief for that brilliant man who has already begun to forget all that he'd been and done and those he has loved. And for our children and me who have to go on without him.

I wonder, too, why it is George who is felled by dementia. I mean, the man I've loved all my life, a brilliant physician, could be saving people's eyesight. How does that compare with writing books and playing the piano? In the simplest of terms, my husband's life is worth more than my own. I feel guilty for being, at least for the present, healthy and whole.

In the claustrophobic silence that surrounds me, my mind runs wild with guilty questions. Was I a good wife? Did I make

George's life happy? Was I smart enough, caring enough? Did George know how much I valued everything he did for me and our children? Did I tell him how much I appreciated his kindness, his gentleness, his patience? Did I say "I love you" enough?

I visit George three times a week, listening to National Public Radio on the way, trying to distract myself from the inevitability of what I will find when I knock on the door to his room . . . the increasing sadness and pain of being with him the way he is . . . removed, less and less able to converse, an unfamiliar George in a familiar body.

I take him out for lunch at a restaurant he loves. He orders the same thing each time and is impatient for its arrival. We sit in silence or I talk and he answers as he can . . . either yes . . . no . . . or okay, though I am unsure of how much he understands. When he finishes eating he leaves the table and wanders off and I have to scramble to pay the bill and still keep him in my sight.

Sometimes we walk around the little village and get an ice cream cone or go to the library or stop at a supermarket to buy apples to keep in his room. Then, I take him back. We kiss goodbye and he stands in the parking lot and watches me leave. That is the hardest part of our visit. Watching him watch me as I pull away makes me crazy with grief.

Today's visit is more than difficult. I am frustrated at my inability to find ways to have him understand some things he needs to do to comply with the safety regulations of his facility. The administration is threatening to discharge him if he keeps refusing. I have strong words with a nurse who is unkind to him, and Pooh, who often goes with me, runs out into the parking lot as George and I are saying goodbye and is nearly hit by a car. By the time I leave to catch the ferry I am frazzled. It is late afternoon and I am stuck in traffic because of an air show at the beach. It takes me almost three hours to get home. I sit in the car crying and cursing, banging my fists on the steering wheel and feeling utterly trapped in my life. I eat chocolate and a big bowl of popcorn for dinner while I watch movies in bed, one after the other, until I fall asleep.

I wake up as dawn is breaking and dress for my walk. I am feeling guilty and angry at myself for yesterday's frustration with George, angry at the nurses in his facility who were little or no help, angry at everything being so damned hard. But, I also know that it isn't really what happened yesterday that is eating at me. At the bottom of it is the guilt that I feel because, as I've said before, I have believed all my life that family should take care of family and I cannot care for George at home. It is more than I can handle physically and emotionally. I have gone back on a tenet that I'd lived by and it is hard to face myself in the mirror.

But, even that is not all of it. As I dig a little deeper, I pull up a more corrosive guilt for what goes by the name of Truth. That truth is that I am now making the choice to care for George in a different way. And I am choosing to have a life of my own, whatever it is. I gave for so many years . . . willingly . . . until I wasn't so willing. I was so caught up in my husband's life that I didn't know who I was. As horrible as his diagnosis was and however wrenching it was to part after so many years together . . . our paths have separated and I am now experiencing myself . . . not in relation to anyone else. I have to continue to find out who I really am. And I have to find a way to live with my choice.

It takes all I have within me just to get through today.

B*o*r*e*d

*I*am bored with this sunshine life . . . the scorching heat, the stinging bugs, the nightly cacophony of frogs and crickets, and the growl of gators. I am bored with days of sameness. Bored with people who look and dress alike. Bored with introspection. Bored with cooking and eating alone. Bored with me. I want . . . I want . . . I want . . . autumn leaves, snowstorms, human diversity, excitement, concerts, theater, museums, and good friends I can reach out and touch.

Never Say B*o*r*e*d

The threat to have George leave his facility has turned into an outright rejection of him as an assisted living resident. When I signed him in, I was told he could stay there for the remainder of his life. But it has become clear that the people in charge do not understand his disease, even though I have given them pages and pages of information, which should have been a red flag for me about their incompetence. They have decided that George needs to be placed in their exceedingly small and confining dementia section. I refuse. He is not ready for it. I do, however, believe it is true that he needs a facility devoted only to dementia patients.

Where am I going to find another place where his particular kind of dementia will be understood and where he will not be too confined? All those I've investigated are unsatisfactory and in some cases horrifying. I again consider having him live with me. But, even with the guilt I feel at not caring for him myself, I know beyond knowing that it would not be in his best interest—or in mine. Pick's Disease causes him to want to walk and walk until he is exhausted. I will not be able to control that or keep him safe. And the progression of the disease is causing greater incontinence. Added to all of it, this brilliant man, who could once lecture for hours at a time, is now barely able to speak.

I visit several places I find on the Internet with two of my children. We are all unhappy with what we see; but settle on one very close to my home that has a nice fenced-in area where George can take his walks and be safe. But, we are worried about their lack of security at the front door. Patients can easily slip out of the dementia area without being noticed when visitors enter. But, all the other places are miserably unsatisfactory. And so I decide that instead of visiting him three times a week, I will try to be there every day, and make certain to take him out for longer walks so that he doesn't feel confined.

Once George is settled in, and over the next several months, I have many conversations with the facility's director about the problems that I encounter: lack of adequate security, not enough activities, and inadequate nursing care. Even though I am there often, George leaves unnoticed on several occasions. I am called to talk him back home. He understands little and is unwilling to do other than what he wishes. I have to drive over and look for the caregiver who has gone after him, help find him, and convince George to get in the car with me and bring them both back. I am frustrated. And I remain more vigilant. I also call the facility's corporate headquarters many times to report the dangers and inadequacies. I am told things will improve. They do not. I know that I will have to find yet another place for George as soon as possible. But circumstances delay my plans.

One afternoon, I discover that George is having problems

urinating. Being a doctor's wife has taught me a few things. I immediately take him to see his doctor. The short of it all is that he is diagnosed with prostate cancer. Options are discussed. Because of his advancing dementia, I choose, with the aid of his doctors, radiation instead of surgery. He has injections and radiation treatment for several months. He is stalwart. In fact, I often think that he might still feel a certain comfort in the hospital setting in which he worked for most of his life. He seems almost happy when we are there.

But, there are moments when I am not sure I will survive what is happening. The cancer treatment has made his incontinence complete. When I take him for his treatments, he soils himself and will not allow me or the nurses to help him. I try to make him understand that I cannot take him to the cafeteria where he likes to get cookies unless his clothes are changed. But he walks away, pulling me where he wants to go. He is a big man and it takes all I can do to coax him back to the car with promises that I will buy him a cookie on the way home.

The radiation treatments come to an end. I see George almost every day, making certain he is not having any adverse affects from the therapy. He is tired and does not want to walk around much. We go for drives and ice cream. There is a kind of lull in the activity of the past months, for which I am grateful.

And then, one night at about ten o'clock, I receive a call. George is missing. No one has seen him since dinner. No one checked on him is what I suspect. I go to his facility. My daughter's boyfriend goes with me. We call the police. They institute a search, including one by helicopter. We drive around the area, looking everywhere we can, showing a picture of George to clerks in stores and asking if he'd been there. I eventually go home and wait and pray. About 3:00 A.M. I am called. He has been found by a young couple at the beach, having walked about ten miles over a major highway. He was in the middle of the road, face down . . . asleep. I ask if he needs medical attention. They say no . . . that he has only a few little bruises . . . and they are cleaning him up and putting him to bed.

After prayers of thanks, I get angry. At the director of the facility, the staff, and at myself for having put him there. I go to see George early the next morning. I look at the "few little bruises" on his legs and arms, which are gashes and tears in his skin and there are insect bites all over him. I just hold his hands and cry and cry. I have serious words with the director. I tell him that I am going to report him and everything else that I have found there to whatever agencies I can find that can do something about the negligence, and to an ombudsman, and to the police, and to a lawyer; and that I will be taking George out of there as soon as I can find a proper facility for him. Corporate headquarters orders a sitter to stay with George twenty-four hours a day. I call lawyers, ombudsmen, police and find out that I would be fighting a losing battle because George was not harmed or dead and that it would be an expensive battle and in the end I would probably lose. Did I really feel up to that? The injustice, the guilt, and the futility are overwhelming. But, the director of George's facility and the corporate executive I had been complaining to are both fired. A little feather.

I think about giving up my condo and finding a larger place where George and I could live with help and where I could keep him safe. But I realize how impossible that life would be now. And that I could never be certain that he *would* be safe.

I immediately visit other dementia facilities and one is worse than the next. I am dejected. Then, a friend in Southern California tells me about one that she has heard is state-of-the-art and not far from her home. She visits it and says they have sent me a video of the facility and what it has to offer George. What the video shows seems the answer to my prayers. I fly out to see for myself. It is everything I ever hoped to find for George. I want this for him, even though it is across the country.

But, given all his difficulties, I do not know how I will be able to transport him on a six-hour plane ride by myself. The problem is solved when the director of the new facility informs me that for the price of his airfare he will come and personally escort George to his new home. There are angels on earth and they appear when you least expect them. I call Rachel, who lives in Northern California. She will fly down to be there to greet her father when he arrives.

In November 2002, George leaves for the airport with the director. He leaves willingly in a taxi, without a nod or a wave. Liz, Carlee, Sammy, and I stand and watch the taxi pull away, hug each other, and cry.

Now What?

After George leaves I am despondent. He is not physically nearby, where at least I can see him and touch him. It is almost like getting the news of his illness all over again. I thought I'd feel relieved to have him living in a safe and wonderfully caring facility, and I do. But I am not prepared for the feelings that are right behind the relief. Guilt rears its worthless head because I have decided not to move to California to be near him. He will be in the perfect place for him to be lovingly cared for and protected. But California is not for me.

I have come to understand that all those months ago, when George asked to go into the assisted living facility and I chose not to, we gave each other the gift of freedom to decide what was next for us and to do what we needed to do for ourselves. My reality and his were separate—and would remain separate. And I am now choosing again . . . the best life for him and for me as well. And so, making the commitment along with my children to visit him regularly, I decide to find a place to live that suits my own wants and needs.

I have been living this new life for almost two years and, in my personal growth, the recognition of who I am and what I want, I find myself thirsting for connection with a cultural life, a creative community . . . community in general. I want to hear live classical music. I want to see plays, and to walk in some of the grandest museums in the world. I want to be in New York City, where the mayor looks like my Uncle Harry. Maybe part of my longing is to return to my roots. I was born in New York City in a Fifth Avenue hospital and I have thought many times about the Native American custom of burying the placenta of newborn babies next to the home so that they always know where home is. Maybe mine is on Fifth Avenue. In any case, I feel drawn to what is familiar. I have fought these feelings for quite a while. Because I knew there was nothing I could do about them but to take short trips to fill myself up with what I've been craving.

As the days pass and I think seriously about leaving Florida, I get very scared. I suddenly acquire a strange, and fortunately benign, heart arrhythmia, have stomach problems, develop tendonitis in both shoulders, arthritis in my right hand and knees, and a myriad of other annoying physical conditions. I say physical, but I am no stranger to the mind/body connection and though I reason that my physical problems are mentally induced, I still run to doctors for comfort and relief. One of them, my internist, looks at me sternly one day and says, "It's obvious that you're depressed. I want you to see a psychiatrist who can recommend an appropriate antidepressant. All these symptoms can be controlled. There's no need for you to feel so terrible." I explain that I have a therapist and that I have tried medication in the past and it has not been good for me. But he persists, saying there are other kinds of medication that I have not tried.

Reluctantly, I make an appointment with the psychiatrist, who turns out to be a kind and compassionate woman who really listens to my story and as well to my desire to feel better without medication. She reiterates my own therapist's early statement to me: "You have a reason to be depressed. What's happened to your husband and yourself is cause enough for anyone to be depressed." And then she says, "But there are other medications you can try that may help you get on with your life." I accept the possibility and take the prescription.

I try the medication for the specified amount of time and hate the way it makes me feel. She tells me to stop taking it and to come in to see her again. I bring her some of my writing and tell her about all the work I have been doing to try to make a new life for myself. During the course of the hour she says to me, "Why are you still in Florida if you want to be in New York?" I say, "Because I'm scared." She then points out to me that it is not unusual for anyone to be scared of a big move and that it is not to be confused with the kind of fear and anxiety that have been my lifelong companions. It makes sense to me. I go home feeling just a little bit closer to taking that leap.

During the next months I begin to formulate a plan to move. I am excited, but also sad. I will be leaving my daughter Liz and my only grandchildren. And . . . I have made my new home a place of comfort and security and I don't want to leave it either. I don't like the idea of anyone else living in my beautiful place, where I have felt so safe and where I have learned how to care for myself alone. But, serendipitously, I meet a single woman who says she would love to rent my place should I decide to move. One by one, obstacles to my leaving are removed. It is time for me to just do it.

One Last Thing

*T*he day I discover my piano is human . . .
that I am not in love with a hunk of black wood with
wire, steel, and plastic for brains, but a breathing,
loving, accepting, and steadfast friend . . . is the day I nearly
lose it to another.

During the trip to New York to find my apartment, I stop
by Steinway Hall. I had read an article about a salesperson
there who seemed to be an expert in finding the perfect piano
for each client. I ask to see her. It has been my lifelong dream
to own a Steinway, preferably one built before World War II,
or a Hamburg Steinway of which there are few in this country.
But more important is that the piano has the sound and touch
that suit me.

I am in luck. The salesperson agrees to see me and takes
me around, asking me questions about my likes and dislikes,
listening to me play on different pianos, and finally, as we part,
she says she is certain she can find me the piano of my dreams.
It is then that I formulate the plan to sell my Yamaha piano . . .
a wonderful instrument but with flaws that cannot be fixed

and that have become a distraction. I will use the money from the sale to put a down payment on a Steinway and finance the rest. I intend to sell my car and this will just be like buying another, expense wise. It will also be cheaper to move without the piano.

Once back in Florida, I find a buyer. A lovely man who is a church choir director. He needs approval from the Board in order to pay my price, which is quite reasonable for the piano's excellent sound and size. When the approval from the Board comes through, but before any final transaction has taken place, I call the saleswoman at Steinway to tell her to start looking for my piano. She doesn't return my phone call. I call again and again, leaving message after message, and never does she call. I am dejected and, as always, when I'm in a *mood*, I sit down at the piano to play.

I will never be able to explain what happens that afternoon at the keyboard. But something mystical passes between the piano and me. In piece after piece, my playing flows as never before. I am in a kind of ecstasy . . . another realm of consciousness. What turns out to be several hours of playing seems like only moments. After the last note of the last piece, I close the lid, put my head on my arms, and sob. This is not just my piano. It is my dearest friend. It has been with me through devastating losses. It has grieved with me, accepted into itself all my pain and sorrow and every moment of every day and night it stands silently, patiently, waiting for me to return to it.

I call a friend and cry, telling her that no matter how much I want a Steinway, the feelings I have for this piano far outweigh what I would receive from owning one. That revelation is at once a disappointment and a joy. My lifelong dream of owning a Steinway is over. But the realization of the value to me of what I *have* is more than compensation for the lost dream. When I finish talking to my friend, I call the choir director and, breaking down several times, tell him what I have discovered. He is so kind and understanding that it makes me feel even more the fact that I have cheated him of his own dream. When I hang up, I go over to the piano and run my hand across its satiny black lid. I think I hear a grand sigh of relief. Or is that me? I go into the kitchen, get a bottle of wine, pour myself a glass, and yes, if you please, I pour one for my piano, set it on top and clink glasses. "To our future life together."

Well . . . hmm! What could possibly come between us after that?

I hire a moving company familiar with New York moves. When they come to estimate the cost, they meet my piano and, knowing they will have to ease it down a flight of stairs and ultimately into an elevator in an apartment building, say they are certain no elevator, especially in an older building like the one I am moving into, could take a piano of that size. I chill to that news and immediately call the rental agent in my apartment house in New York. He doesn't think my piano will fit in the elevator either. I have already signed a two-year lease, committed myself to a move-in date only two weeks away. What am I going to do? I momentarily lose my mind. Because, what I do is call the choir director and tell him what has happened and ask if he would still be interested in buying my piano. He says he will get back to me.

While I wait for his call, I suddenly get my wits back. I pick up the phone and call a piano store in New York City that sells Yamaha pianos like mine and ask what piano movers they use. I call the one recommended and tell them my story.

"Piece o' cake," the piano man says to me. "Don't believe

the movers. They just don't want the responsibility. Tell them to deliver it to us and we'll get it to you."

It is like hearing from the doctor that my newborn baby has all its fingers and toes.

"But . . . wait," I say. "What if they're right . . . and the elevator *is* too small. Would you be willing to go over there and look at it? Pleeeeze, just to be sure?"

"Okay. No problem. Gimme a week."

"Wait, wait," I say. "I have someone who wants to buy the piano but I don't want to sell it. Can you get over there in a day or two?"

"See what I can do. Call me Wednesday."

"You promise? You don't know how important this is to me."

"Promise . . . promise. Don't worry, sweet-haht," he says, his Bronx accent comforting my heart.

I am now kicking myself for having called the choir director before this brainstorm hit. I hope he will not call back before I know if I can actually take my beloved piano with me. I am not remotely prepared to think of what it will feel like if I have to watch it leave my home, now that I know what I know about the bond we share. But, the director calls and says the church is still interested. I then have to tell him what has happened. As good a man as I know him to be, I think he will certainly hang up on me, if not worse. But, he doesn't. Once again, he says he understands my predicament and to just call when I know what I am going to do. Another angel in my path.

Three anxiety-filled days later, I call the piano mover in New York. I ask him if he's been to my apartment house and seen the service elevator. I suck in my breath and wait. "Yeah. The guys went yesterday. It's nine feet high. No problem!" I bless him, his family, his company, and his entire future on the planet. I call the local mover and make arrangements for the piano to be dropped off in the Bronx and for the piano movers to deliver it to my apartment.

And then, I call the choir director. He wishes me well and says I did the right thing for me, and that is important. I love him and bless him and his church and his mother for having had such a son. I give out a lot of blessings this day; but it is I who feel truly blessed by the fates and everyone who had been a part of helping me out of my near disaster.

I sit down to play, to soothe my piano's aching heart and mine. I beg its forgiveness for my temporary insanity. "Fagedaboudit," it says . . . preparing itself for New York. But . . . crazy I am . . . crazy in love with my imperfectly perfectly wonderful piano.

I will never let it go. And it knows now that I speak the truth.

Time to Go

The apartment I find in New York City is small but it has wonderful views of the East River, and to the north and west of the city. I can watch boats sail by, planes flying into LaGuardia Airport, and at night the dazzling lights of high-rise apartments and also the George Washington Bridge lit up like a green tiara. It is not only the view that attracts me to what is to be my new home, but also the fact that my piano can have its own space in what ordinarily would be a small dining room. And more than that . . . I can afford to live there for several years.

This tropical life has been easy . . . boring but easy. But I am not looking for easy. I want a soul-filling life. And so, I know that I have to take another leap into the future I am creating for myself. I am scared, that's for certain. I also have no illusions that things will miraculously change for me by changing my place of living. I take me with me wherever I go. I just want to experience *me* in New York City. I am sixty-six and I have to do it now. It is a wrenching decision to leave my daughter and grandchildren; but if I don't get out of my comfort zone and trust what my soul is telling me to do, I know that one day I will look back and say, "Coulda . . . shoulda done it."

I leave for New York City with my little dog, Pooh, in August of 2003.

My first night in my new bedroom, boxes all around me, the lights of the city brightening the room, I say a prayer of thanks . . . to more people than I can name . . . and also to myself. I had the courage to take a chance on me. I am not afraid. I am not anxious. I am not depressed. I am excited and happy, even though I am very much . . . a*l*o*n*e.

My Home, Beautiful Home 2

I *am finally unpacked. Again. I would live* well with half of what I've put away; and in time I will most assuredly let go of more things.

As I sit in my living room on this hazy Indian summer day, the air conditioning humming, my apartment, with its New York white walls, suddenly speaks to me. What it says is that in this city of horns, sirens, concrete, and a few pop-up trees, I need to create again a warm personal sanctuary. I find that, rather than being exhausted after the move and all the putting away, I am excited at the prospect of transforming these few rooms into a home. Immediately, I know that I want bold color this time around . . . red . . . golden yellow . . . the reflection of a different me . . . a different mood for a different time.

There are many pluses about living in an apartment house. Lots of people around to talk with, to fix whatever is needed, to deliver packages to the door. I find a very helpful porter who says he will paint my apartment on his days off. Over the next few weeks, I am in and out of the paint store up the street, and looking for shops that sell window coverings. Soon I've made all my selections.

The porter and his friend paint the entire apartment on a Saturday and take down the misshapen window blinds. The new shades are installed. They give a lovely finish to the rooms and through them I am still able to see the lights of the city at night.

I am happy. My small, colorful, new home . . . crowded again with personal treasures, reflected aspects of myself . . . woman, daughter, wife, mother, artist, musician, liver of life. I have carried with me the books I love most that speak to all my interests—literature, spirituality, music, writing, art, biographies of women who made it alone and who, through hard times and perseverance managed to contribute much to the world. And on the shelves that hold these books, a myriad of memories—saved greeting cards; candles; jacks and pick-up sticks, games of my own childhood that I played with my grandchildren; and a photo of the little girl who was me, and for whom I write. On the computer, now a part of my bedroom, still the Barbie doll shoe, the fertility god, the rubber chicken, the rose, and above it a full bowl of white shells which, every so often, I pour onto my bed and hold in my hands, remembering how important those morning walks on the beach were to my feeling of well-being.

For the final touch . . . and to counteract Big Apple concrete, I once again need green. On most every corner in New York City there are flower shops with good prices, so I can make myself happy for not a lot of money. I buy more plants and keep small vases of fresh flowers in every room. On the many gray New York days, they will be my sunshine.

And so, in my journey to the center of the bed, I have created two very special places for myself. I have no doubt that I could and would do it again if I have the need or if circumstances dictate. But I am more than content here and now. I love living in this city and in this home . . . looking around me and seeing mementos of my life as it grew into what it is today.

And yet, perhaps strange to say, some of the most special times for me are when I return home from wherever my day has taken me. I stand a block away and look up at my apartment and the warm and comfortable place I have made for myself. When I see the lamps that I have lit for my homecoming, I am happily aware that I am both the someone away and the someone waiting to welcome me home and I have such feelings of joy in going back to the place where my sweet, nervous little dog waits, and where both of us, in just a few moments, will feel the safety and security of each other in our home . . . beautiful home.

Pooh

I live in a section of New York City called Yorkville. I live on York Avenue and I have a Yorkie named Pooh . . . a six-pound, spoiled-rotten dog with super intelligence and an imperial personality. He is referred to by my friend Calla as The Prince of York; and by me, for his loyalty and constant love, as my little hairy husband.

I think of him as human, until he eats something disgusting in the street. He hates other dogs. He wags his tail, and then bites them. If he is in my arms and thinks I am being threatened, he will chew on whoever is trying to pet him. He has a bad reputation in my building.

He is fickle. If I leave him with Calla when I go out, he will shun me and run to her. When I come back, he will ignore her and pay attention only to me.

He has bad habits. He is neutered but will try to mate with any stuffed animal he happens to meet. He will eat anything. He has died once . . . from eating poisoned anti-termite pellets around my home in Florida . . . and was revived by an outstanding veterinarian. He was near death a second time when he ate half of my coconut cream birthday cake left on the dining room table.

Pooh remains a large part of the answer as to why I am able to get out of bed in the morning. He has licked away the wounds of my heart. He has comforted me on terror filled nights with his snoring and warm little body huddled next to mine. He has traveled with me . . . badly, has trained me to fetch and carry for him. He has severe separation anxiety, and craves company even when he eats. I sit on the floor with him . . . he sits at my side when I dine in. We are getting crotchety and achy as we grow old together. We are the same age in dog years. Above all, he has made me aware that I can still love . . . deeply.

And, too often, I find myself looking into his round, sweet, brown eyes and begging, "Please, my darling little Pooh, don't ever leave me. Let's go together. I don't want to live without you."

Big Apple Blues

My life is like the tracings of a cardiogram. Up. Down. Up again. Down again. Peaks and valleys. One day . . . or maybe if I'm lucky . . . a few days in a row . . . I'm happy and serene. The next . . . sad and lonely. Moving to New York City is not a cure for loneliness. I didn't believe it would be. But, it has greatly improved the quality of my life because there are so many choices of things I love to do. And there are many others doing things alone as well. I don't feel like I'm wearing a yellow dress at a red party.

However, I wasn't aware of some of the emotions living here would produce, because New York City feels like home. These are my people, my geographic family. I grew up in New Jersey, went to college in New York, and lived in Brooklyn with my husband when he was in medical school and specialty training. We spent a lot of time in Manhattan.

When I walk the streets to reacquaint myself with the city, everywhere I go my eyes rest on couples walking, talking, laughing, eating at outdoor cafes together, and I am overcome with intense loneliness. I want to say, "Talk to me, please. Invite me to sit with you. Someone, see me!" I am a lonely eight-year-old again. And when I am in Central Park and in front of me is an elderly couple holding hands, supporting each other as they make their way down the path, I am in tears. Worst of all is seeing an aged woman with a cane or one being led by a caregiver. I don't see her. I see myself, my future, and run for home.

I've spent so much time finding within me the courage to move on with my life alone, I haven't realized how much part of me still wants to be the other half of a couple. How much I want to be loved and cherished the way I had been. To say again, "How was your day, honey?" And to hear the answer. Until my husband was lost to me, I never knew how much I wanted to share myself and to have someone share himself with me. The value of that sharing, how much brighter life seems when there are two. The fears that can be softened when there is someone next to you to help or counsel or just listen without judgment.

But there is no other one anymore. And there may never be another love in my life. And so, I have to sit still and bear those thoughts, those moments of agonizing loneliness, and the aching for lost love and know that those times will come and they will go. There is no way to sidestep them.

There is another truth that I have to acknowledge . . . the other side of loneliness: how much I value my solitude. Because it is in that solitude that I create, I think and dream, I read and learn. And there, I am never lonely. And so, if it is my destiny to live out my days as I live them now, I will be grateful for the opportunity given to me by the circumstances of my life. Loneliness included.

I will not let the lonely times shake my resolve to make

it alone . . . in every sense of the word. To make my own happiness, different to be sure, but fulfilling without a partner. I *have* to do it. Because my life still has meaning . . . other than being wife, mother, grandmother. The kind of meaning that comes from directing my own days and nights. I have value to myself and things to offer to the world still. I do not know what the future will give me. But whatever it is, and if I continue on alone, then I will still have me. And every day the knowledge of that me is a greater source of strength and appreciation.

So, I read the Sunday *Times* and tag all the things I want to do and make myself call for one ticket. I go to the theatre alone. I go to my Carnegie Hall subscription series alone. At first it feels strange, as if the spotlight is on me and everyone in the audience is staring at me and thinking, "Oh look, a woman alone." Then, as I look around me, I see many women by themselves. And when I board the bus that takes me home, it is filled with women alone. We are a kind of sorority of solitary women. I look at them and wonder about their stories. What magic has life worked to bring them alone to this bus on this night? I feel a sadness for all of us and also a kinship and awareness that I am not unique. I am simply me, out on the town, doing what I love to do, and trying to learn to love it no less because I am alone.

The Hall That Andrew Built

*A*s *I move through my new life in New York* City I am living more deliberately, aware of every effort I make in my own behalf, aware of the progress I make some days. And though on other days I am exhausted by all the effort, wishing I didn't have to try so hard, that things would just come to me, those feelings are short-lived. Because this new ability to reach out for the things I want and need feels good, feels comfortable, feels like me. And what I come to know is that because I am continuing to follow my heart, fabulous opportunities are opening to me, opportunities that are helping me to become more of the woman I'm meant to be. The sad irony is that they would not have happened at all but for the strange twist my life took.

This next one, most particularly.

I make a promise to myself. To finish the two books I've been working on before I ever think of moving again.

But, as the days move forward, I understand that given what I love to do most, write and play the piano, I might never leave my apartment. I would like to meet new people and also volunteer my time to something that has meaning for me.

I think about why I moved to New York City . . . the excitement of being able to go to concerts, plays, museums . . . all that I have been missing for many years. And then, I know. I call Carnegie Hall and find that they have a volunteer program. I am invited for an interview, during which I am asked if I'd like to become a docent, giving tours to the public. Oh, yes . . . I would!

Over the next few months, I learn about the history of the Hall, the man who built it, and the long list of artists who have performed there. I love the learning. But . . . I have to commit to memory so much material. I'm getting older. Will I remember it all? And I haven't done any public speaking for a very long time. I could embarrass myself. What if my tour group asks questions and I don't know the answers? What if I trip up the stairs? Or down? What if I fall over the balcony? I think I am in elementary school again.

After my last training class, I am told that in order to qualify, I will have to give a tour to my teacher and the head of the volunteer program. I am as nervous as my Yorkie. But, I pass the test. More daunting than that test is the fact that I am now on my own, free to sign up to guide as many tours as I wish. I get my security badge and I am officially a Carnegie Hall Volunteer.

I schedule myself for my first tour, sleep poorly the night before, and am too nervous to eat breakfast before I leave. I arrive at the Hall and go to the volunteer office to check in. No one is there. The room is dark. I call around and find that all tours have been cancelled that day. Someone neglected to tell me. I breathe a sigh of relief, but what I do next turns out to be something that will remain in my memory forever.

I decide to take the keys and explore the Hall . . . alone.

I try the first key that opens the door from the Museum into the Hall. The lock is tricky, but I try several times until I understand its little secret. I take the elevator up to the Dress Circle . . . walk up to the balcony and into the Hall. The lights are dimmed, yet its red plush seats clearly visible. This wonderful, enormous balcony Andrew Carnegie created to ensure that those as poor as he'd been as a child could afford to attend a concert . . . thirty-five cents in the front rows, twenty-five in the rear . . . in 1891.

I look down on the dark stage. There is only the ghost . . . a bright light on a pole that burns throughout the night when the stage is dark . . . placed there because of old superstitions . . . to ward off ghosts of performances past . . . as well as for safety. I sit awhile, breathing in the dark and pulsing silence, aware of the smallness of myself in this grandest of concert halls. Then, I move slowly down the stairs to the Dress Circle, named for those social folk of the late 1800s who came in their very best garments to see and be seen. I walk its perimeter and then down to the first row, where I will start my tours. I sit, my arms on the railing, and look up at the ceiling and the circle of ninety-six lights . . . then down into the boxes of the First and Second Tiers with their moveable chairs and little cloak rooms and then climb the steep steps back to the elevator.

I exit at the Parquet level, the orchestra level in other halls, walk up the steps to look at the bust of Andrew Carnegie, and have a quiet conversation with him. He tells me he's happy that I'm there and to please continue.

I enter the auditorium and sit directly in the center. My skin crawls with excitement. There are no technicians, no stagehands, no cleaning staff. I am the only one in the Hall.

Suddenly, I hear music . . . so much music . . . music of the last century, music of today, cascading from the iron and steel and plaster. I imagine opening night, ladies in their elegant dresses with leg of mutton sleeves, large plumed hats, and delicate evening purses. Gentlemen in frock coats and top hats. I turn to see Mr. Carnegie, dressed in black, tipping his own top hat to the audience in his rose garlanded box, number 33, and turn back to watch Pyotr Ilyich Tchaikovsky conducting the orchestra. I see Vladimir Horowitz trying to find exactly the right spot for his piano. I see Arthur Rubenstein in his tuxedo, head proud, hands flying. I hear Maria Callas and Ella Fitzgerald. I hear Benny Goodman's clarinet and see men and women dancing in the aisles. I watch Leonard Bernstein take up his baton the afternoon of his debut. I hear the Beatles and the screaming girls. And then . . . pandemonium, as Issac Stern lifts his violin to play to an audience that rises as one, clapping and shouting its tribute to the man who saved Carnegie Hall from destruction and to whom this auditorium is dedicated. I can hardly breathe. The past is so close.

Finally, I walk down to the white-oak stage floor and gaze above me at the proscenium arch, the tiara of lights, and turn to look back into the empty seats, imagining what it would be like to be a star performer, seeing the anticipation in the faces of those filling the Hall just for me . . . and knowing I had the talent to give them the best musical evening of their lives. I stand for a long time with my eyes closed. I have a difficult time pushing myself toward the exit. For the last hour there has been only the sound of my own footsteps and yet I have heard a thousand concerts.

When the Director of Volunteers calls to apologize for not having told me that my tours were cancelled, I thank him for forgetting.

I give my first tours to great numbers of children on spring break, bleary eyed from being on buses the entire night. They stagger, sleep against the walls, talk to each other, and are totally disinterested in all the wonderful information I have to share. But the good news is that I am gaining confidence in myself . . . and my memory.

I am now a veteran docent. I give walk-in tours on Mondays with a sister docent named Lillian who has also become a lovely friend. We welcome people from all over the world and from every state in this country. They ask wonderful and ridiculous questions. We laugh a lot, lunch together, and when the Hall is closed for a week or for the summer months, we confess to each other our worry that we won't remember what to say. That has never happened.

And on those Mondays, when I direct my groups down to stage front, I ask them not to turn around until they have arrived there. Then, I stand aside and wait to hear them as they have their first look into the Hall before them. Always, always, there are great sighs and murmurs of "Oh . . . how beautiful." And then, I am happy. For they have truly appreciated the greatness of the place I have loved for all of my life . . . the place where I feel most alive . . . most myself . . . the Hall that Andrew Carnegie built.

I make another promise to myself: one day, when there is a piano waiting for the evening's performer, I will ask permission to walk up on the stage and play . . . just one short piece . . . and turn toward box number 33 and say, "This was my dream. And here I am, awake, and playing in my beloved Carnegie Hall. Thank you, Mr. Carnegie. Blessings on you, forever."

Drowning

*I*t is said that when you're drowning your entire life flashes before your eyes. It's true. I was sixteen and too far from shore.

No longer floundering in a roiling ocean, I still, on occasion, feel like I am drowning in the sea of my own memories, helpless to pull myself up and out . . . only able to give in. The loss of my husband is not easier as the days move further from our parting. Perhaps because he is alive . . . but not alive . . . here . . . but not here. Time is not healing the wound of his illness and our separation. The wound gapes as I age without him.

I sit on a bench in Central Park on the first sweet-crisp day of autumn. I don't want to think. I don't want to remember. But it is the very air, the cool smoky atmosphere of this day, that draws me back and back. George, in his heavy blue sweater, his eyes bright with the love of his favorite season. He reaches for my hand as we kick at the fragrant golden leaves and laugh like our children. I look up at him, his cheeks red, his mouth in a ready smile. I squeeze his hand with my own joy and contentment.

These are Monday's memories. They come from a life well lived and loved. But more than ever, I am aware of the empty space beside me. The life I have made for myself has its own richness now. Would I give it up if I could reach out and take my husband's hand and walk with him in the beauty of this autumn day? Today . . . I would.

The Little Black Bird of Depression

I have a beautiful coat. It is an indoor coat, created and stitched by my friend Pat Brown, a gifted seamstress. The coat is of many colors . . . a black/red/green paisley fabric with gold lamé patches depicting the sun and moon . . . and the word *abracadabra* sewn in colored letters in a triangle of small tan squares across the back, each line eliminating the last letter of the word until there is only the letter A left. What is most extraordinary about my quilted coat is that on the left shoulder sits a stuffed, black, cotton bird with small black beady eyes.

Pat informed me that the coat has magic in it. After I purchased it, some ten years ago, I wore it every time I sat down to write, hoping the magic would manifest in my writing. These days, its significance in my life has deepened and I wrap myself in my abracadabra coat for a different reason.

In ancient times, the letters in the word *abracadabra* were often printed on a piece of parchment and worn around the neck. The configuration of these letters was supposed to act like a funnel to drive dis-ease out of the body.

ABRACADABRA

ABRACADABR

ABRACADAB

ABRACADA

ABRACAD

ABRACA

ABRAC

ABRA

ABR

AB

A

The little bird, that raven or crow that sits on my shoulder, has become for me the black bird of my own dis-ease . . . or more correctly . . . depression. It is never outside my view. I can sniff its presence, hear its caw, and feel the beating of its shiny wings against my cheek. But the coat to which it is attached has come to be a wrap of transformation. Together they form a part of the costume of humanity that I wear.

Depression is often described as black. Also bad, fearsome, dark, evil. Those adjectives aptly describe what depression feels like . . . in part. I'd also include sorrowful, hopeless, and debilitating. No one wants to be depressed. There are degrees of depression for certain, but once at the bottom of one, it would be fair to say none of us would wish to go there again. Depression is frightening because once in, it feels like there is no way out.

I find no nobility in suffering and if there were a pill to lessen my pain, I'd surely take it. But medication has never made me feel anything but worse. So, I've had to swear off and tough out the depressions with the help of my therapist and my symbolic coat of many colors.

Depressions for me have come, in the main, from life circumstances. But I also know that depression holds tight hands with the creative personality. Described as moody as a child, what I certainly was feeling was depression, though never really taken seriously or diagnosed as such. Through the years, I have had more than my share of life situations to produce depression. I felt I had no life tools to cope with illness, loss, death—and yet, there they were, and I had to deal with them. I stuffed my feelings, fears, and anxieties inside until, one by one, my seams gave way, everything I'd hidden began to leak out and I experienced depression.

Most of my depressions were caused by deaths in the family. None were lingering deaths. Not that I would want a loved one to suffer, but what I mean is that I never had a chance to say goodbye. Most of the people I loved succumbed suddenly to failure of the heart. Grandmother, mother, brother, aunts, uncles. Dearest ones. My father committed suicide in my home, unable to bear any longer his terrible disease of laryngeal cancer. I never had the chance to make things come right that were not. No chance to express deep love and appreciation for life and love given. And not surprisingly, depression has accompanied my grief at the loss of my husband while having to watch his deterioration into oblivion.

But what I've learned from depression I may not have been able to learn any other way. To be sure, it is a tough way to have to learn anything. First and foremost, I have learned not to fight it, but to accept that it is there and to wrap myself, figuratively and sometimes literally, in my coat of transformation. There is no modern magician, wand in hand, shouting "Abracadabra!" and whoosh . . . depression gone. What is mine to do is to work my way through. I have to stay with it, explore its depths, its messages, its formidable hold on my life . . . until there is a shift, a thumbnail of brightness, the depression begins to lighten, and finally lift. The journey back to wholeness often takes months. Having the patience to be supremely uncomfortable for a long period of time is now a fact of my life. "The reward of patience is patience," said St. Augustine. But it is anything but easy.

I am always interested in finding metaphors for depression. One day, my dear friend Paula, artist/writer/weaver, told me about the black that is produced from the mixing of all colors together. Viewing the blackness of my depression as the end result of all the bright and beautiful colors of my life that have temporarily run together, gives me yet another way to think of it and to give it more meaning. My depression as an art form . . . a colorful and original painting found again by a deft hand that has carefully cleared away an overlay of black. Certainly, it is easier to think in those terms when I am not depressed; but when I am, it also helps me to keep my eye on that original work of art that is my true life.

I've learned more from being at the bottom than by trying to avoid slathering down into the muddy pit. And that awareness has recently made me rethink my fears that depression will return. Now I look upon my little black bird as a life companion, who at times tries to get me to pay attention to things I need to know. The most important of which is to stay aware and deal with the situations that are prone to bring me to the edge before they do. Pay attention to what I am thinking and feeling . . . what is happening not only on the outside of my life but what I am making of it in my inner world. I so often wish to be the "happy carrot" that author and Jungian analyst Marion Woodman talks about . . . unconscious, asking no questions . . . just vegging out and accepting everything as fate. But, I am no happy carrot. Though it is painful, and fraught with anxiety . . . I am bound to my quest for self-understanding and growth. And so, at times, I must wear my abracadabra coat, listen to the messages of my little black bird, and wrap myself in the knowing that I will come through again.

Mom, Mama, Mommy

A wise old friend once told me, "The best thing you can do for your children is the best thing you can do for yourself." That message has guided my thinking since she said it. Because martyrdom produced an angry mother for me, I vowed not to let that happen to my children's mother.

When our children were young, not many mothers worked outside the home. I had a traditional role. George was free to pursue the work he loved as I took care of him, our children, and our home. I cooked, was good at it; cleaned . . . was so bad at it that George once remarked that he didn't really mind that I wasn't good at keeping house, but he was afraid that some of the dust bunnies would roll down the stairs and kill one of the children. I did the laundry, drove the children to music lessons, dentists, pediatricians, planned and executed birthday parties, was a den mother, a band parent, helped with homework, and tucked them all into bed at night. I found time to teach piano, play tennis, and join organizations of interest to me; but I was always home when they came home from school. I made after-school snacks and baked cookies for classroom parties.

What was most important to me as I traveled the motherhood road was not to duplicate the things I did not like about my own childhood. Sadly, I was not always successful. There were things I did that I cannot believe I did . . . like not speaking to my children when I was angry at them . . . just as I had been ignored . . . and once, heaven help me, I washed Liz's mouth out with soap. I was a sassy child and got that a lot. But doing it to my own child was mindless. And sad to think there may be other things I did that I have pushed into forgetfulness. It was when I finally woke up to having enough confidence in myself to follow my own mothering instincts that I became the mother I wanted to have myself. My fondest desire was to make certain my children knew that I was someone they could count on to be there for them in any way they needed me.

When I was discussing the fact that I wanted to write something in this book about my motherhood, Liz said what she remembers above all is that I always made her feel precious and beautiful, especially when she did not feel particularly good about herself. I must have done some things right after the soap incident for her to be able to say that. And, because I came away from my own home life with severe self-doubt that has taken a lifetime to overcome, those were glorious words to hear.

When the children were older and my father was acutely ill with cancer and living with us, I went back to school to get my master's degree in music. I had some help in the afternoons, so they were all well tended and I could feel secure about leaving a few afternoons a week. Even though I wasn't always there when the children got home, under the glass dome in the kitchen were pieces of my love for them in the form of brownies, peanut butter logs, or Rice Krispie bars with chocolate icing.

Rachel said to me recently, "I loved seeing those treats for us because your message to me was 'I love you, and I have my own goals to pursue, too.' You were a role model for me because taking the time to bake before you went to class said that you cared for me and you cared for yourself." What she didn't know until much later in her life was that I didn't feel like a model for anything except maybe the ability to escape. I went back to school as a defense against watching my father, my hero, die slowly in front of my eyes. I still had to have the energy to care for my family while my heart was breaking. So I tried to save myself by studying and practicing so that for just a few hours a day I didn't have to think about what was happening in my home.

I was often a lonely mother, because George was extremely busy with his work and away from home a great deal. The children were used to his chair at the dining table being empty on many occasions and took it in stride. One day, our daughter Rachel walked into the center of town after school with her friend Becky. Something flew into Becky's eye. She tried to get it out, but Rachel, having absorbed much information from her father, admonished her not to. If my memory serves me well, their conversation went something like this:

"Don't rub your eye, Becky. You can do a lot of damage."

"But, it hurts. I need to get it out."

"Let's take the bus to see my dad in the clinic. He'll get it out."

So, the two of them took the bus to the hospital clinic and Rachel went to the desk and said to the assistant, "Hi, I'm Rachel Weinstein. Dr. Weinstein's daughter. My friend has something in her eye and we need to see my dad."

Said the assistant, "Your dad's been in California for a week."

Because George was away so much, when he returned and took his place at the head of the table, the children, unused to his presence, still directed most of their conversation to me. Even when they had a medical question, an ache or pain . . . they'd sing out. . . "Mom, I have a sore throat." Or "Mom, I have this weird thing on my foot, will you take a look?" I had to remind them that Dr. Dad was home and those questions could now be answered by someone really in the know. George took all this with his usual good humor.

Each of our children has a unique personality, preferences, and abilities. All of them have worried me, and tried my patience and understanding as they grew and tried to separate from the warm nest provided them. I've always tried to recognize their differences; but I still can't remember who hates eggplant and who hates mushrooms. Thank goodness none of them is allergic to nuts. I made a lot of mistakes. But I loved them while I was making those mistakes. And I think they always knew that. I tended to over-shelter; but, about that, Rachel said to me, "Mom, I'd rather have been over protected than not cared about at all." There *is* a happy medium. I don't think I ever found it.

In any case, they have all turned out to be beautiful, interesting, productive people, with their share of problems to solve as have we all. I have seen them through their life crises; bad choices in boyfriends and girlfriends; employment problems; a difficult marriage, which happily, however, produced two of the greatest joys of my life, my grandchildren; and a divorce. My children and I have had our share of upsets, disagreements, angry withdrawals—and, as we all matured, a coming together as adults. I am variously called *Mom* or

Mama, and when I pick up the telephone and hear one of them say "Hi, Mommy" I know immediately that some tender loving care is needed. Fortunately, motherhood comes with a lifelong supply.

But it is on the occasions when we visit George and I watch our children as they gently care for their father, walk with him, talk to him, smooth his hair, massage his hands with cream, tears lining their faces, that I am overcome with pride at the tender, loving people they have become. Because I also know the sadness beneath their sadness . . . that they can never resolve what was left between them and their father. They have had to make peace with the incomplete. But, I am still here to help them know what I know . . . how much their father cherished each one of them and to tell them all the things he said to me over the years, but, perhaps, never to them.

With George's diagnosis of dementia, all of our lives changed forever, separately and as a family. But, our love and care for each other has grown stronger and more palpable. My children have been very much my cheerleaders in my quest to find a life of my own, even when I knew that my daughter Liz and grandchildren were despondent about my move away from where we had started our Florida life together. And they all have been my strongest supports in my struggle to do the best I can for their father.

My daughters and I talk almost every day. My son, Bruce, and I not as often. He lives a block away; but is out of town a great deal. We email and speak when we can, have dinner, go to movies, and other events together. He will marry the love of his life in a few weeks and move to Brooklyn. The morning after one of his engagement parties, I told him how thrilled I am that he is able to experience such great love in his lifetime, and to have such a beautiful relationship with his soon-to-be-wife, Kristen. He said to me, "It's because of you and dad and what I saw in my home. I saw the love and the kindness and caring you showed each other. I know things weren't always good between you but I always saw love." His words are a profound gift.

In my difficult times I try not to unload my sadness or loneliness; but my children hear my voice and they know. Just as I hear theirs and know. We support each other mightily as we walk this new path. And, not surprisingly when we are together, we revert to the roles of their childhood, although with adult intelligence and articulation. We know it. We laugh about it, but now there is support and love for each other that shines through any old "stuff" that comes through. They have grown up. I have grown up. We have become the best of friends. I have tried to let go and to see them as adults who do not need or want advice from me, unless they ask. Sometimes, I actually succeed.

And on those rare occasions when all of us are able to gather around a dinner table, George's empty chair, too visible, we always toast him with the remembrance of the love he had for us and the power of his presence in our lives. And then, we celebrate the wonderful fact that we still have each other.

Hands Down

I never imagined anything happening to my hands . . . anything besides aging arthritic joints . . . anything that would prevent me from playing the piano or tapping at my computer keys. But suddenly, the fingers of my right hand are incredibly painful and tend to stay in a bent position until I gently raise them up again. It is almost impossible to practice the piano or to write.

I have developed what the hand surgeon tells me are *trigger fingers*. He injects cortisone into the tendons. It helps for a few months, during which time I give an in-home recital that I have been working on for a long time. All the practicing has greatly added to the pain in my hand and the triggering returns. I decide to have surgery to release the tendons in all five fingers of my right hand.

It is not a wonderful experience. I am afraid of anesthesia. Opt not to have it; but, according to the surgeon, I ask for it when I am sedated. The residue, the coming awake, and the sick feeling from all the medication is hard to shake. But a few days after the surgery I am feeling better and glad to have it over and done with. I have a large bandage on my hand for a week. The stitches are removed and I undergo painful rehabilitative therapy for several months until my hand function and strength are restored. For the skill of my surgeon and my complete recovery, I am truly grateful.

Several months later, the fingers of my left hand begin to trigger. I am bereft. I return to my surgeon and over the next months have the maximum number of injections allowed. He tells me I need surgery again. I tell him that I am trying to finish my writing projects and want to wait and see how much I can do before pain or dysfunction interfere. He tells me that the longer I wait the longer it will take to get my fingers back to normal. But I am not ready. I soak my hands. I use splints and take anti-inflammatory medication when the pain gets too bad. I do well enough. I can type and play the piano . . . though not pieces that demand ultimate dexterity or power. I will try to finish my work before I decide what to do. It is now one year later and I still have not had the surgery.

But, this experience has changed me. When I look at my hands, I see them not as freckled, veined, aging, and slightly arthritic appendages, but rather as the keys to my creative process. My tools. The translators of my thoughts, emotions, musical instincts, and understanding. My hands nourish my heart and soul as much as they help me nourish my body when they pick up knife and fork and feed me. And, now that I am paying them close attention, I have added them in particular to my list of what I am grateful for in my life. Whatever my daily prayer, it always begins with *"Thank you for the miracle of my hands."*

The Artist is On The Table

My physical therapist has an office in one of the studio towers at Carnegie Hall that houses people in various artistic professions. His name is Shmuel Tatz. He is world renowned for his magical work, which he calls *body tuning*, with famous dancers, pianists, and musicians of all kinds. Finding him is a great blessing in my arthritic and muscle-aching life. His studio is unlike any other. I open the door and enter a peaceful world. Irina, a serenely beautiful assistant, sits at her desk . . . the only sound is classical music playing in the background. Lights are dim, talking is at a minimum between Shmuel, his staff, and patients.

I relax even before I lie down on his professional table. As our sessions progress, I tell him a little about myself and ask about him and his career. Soon we are talking music and I am greatly impressed by his breadth of knowledge of music and performers. I find out, too, that he has written a book titled *The Pianist's Hands*. I tell him that I am a pianist and I show him my hands, the one that had surgery and the one that is still ailing. I tell him my piano playing is not what it once was; but that I can still play. He takes my hands in his and presses here, there, shakes his head, and says with his thick Lithuanian accent, "Poor you. You cannot play with these hands."

The next week I bring him a recording of my master's piano recital, of which all these years later I am still proud. It was one of the highlights of my life, a time like few others when I stretched myself to my limits. He accepts my CD and thanks me. When I return the next week, I wonder if he has listened to it; but I am not comfortable asking. He is a straight shooter. I am a little afraid of his critique. So, I say nothing. He works on my neck and shoulders and suddenly, my recording begins to play. I say, "Oh, my goodness. You're playing it for everyone to hear?"

He says, "Yes. It is wonderful." As he continues to work on my body, the music plays on.

Our session ends. Shmuel tells me to rest for awhile. I continue to listen to my recording as I lie there. Up comes a Haydn Sonata and I am amazed at how my fingers could fly the way they did way back then. Suddenly the curtain that separates me from the next patient he is working on is drawn back quickly. Shmuel says to me, "This is perfection." And he closes the curtain.

I have goose bumps. I lie still until the Sonata ends. The audience on my CD is clapping for me. And now Shmuel is by my side, saying to everyone in the studio, "Please, everybody, clap! The artist is on the table!" And he points to me.

A young woman who has hurt her ankle is hanging from a contraption in the ceiling while moving a ball around with her feet. "Is that really you playing?" she says.

"Yes," I say.

She slips gently down to the floor. "That's fantastic!"

"Thanks," I say. "You've all made my day!"

I want to lie there and listen to the rest of my recording; but I get myself up slowly. I am relaxed and also highly energized by what has happened this morning. I find my coat and hat. Shmuel says, "You are not staying to hear the rest of your performance?" I tell him I have to give a tour of the Hall. He says, "Well then, you must go, but your spirit will stay here with us." I hug him and thank him for what he did for me that day. He says, "I know if you did not choose your family, you could have big career." I tell him those are the nicest words I have heard in a very long time.

I leave feeling that I had been given a great gift. This afternoon I give one of my best tours in the happiest of moods. With gratitude in my heart for having been that morning . . . the artist on the table.

Carriage Ride, Anyone?

The first warm day of spring. Tourists, native New Yorkers, all enjoying the soft air and budding trees. I am on my way to physical therapy for my ailing neck. I spend too many hours at the computer. A red light stops me at Fifth Avenue and the entrance to Central Park. A line of horses and carriages waits next to me.

"Ride, young lady?" a man says, smiling, pandering to my grey hair. "Howaboutanicetourofthepark . . . greatprice?"

"No, thanks, old boy. I live here."

His smile evaporates. He walks off.

But his horse and I stare at each other. A white horse with a stupid red plume attached to its harness. I am suddenly angry and terribly sad. I hate circuses. I hate zoos. I hate what has happened to this horse. His sad eyes remain fixed on me. And mine on his. And suddenly I am crying. A beautiful horse, bound, trapped, hitched to a carriage, forced to go round and round on black pavement when he should be wild, free, his hooves pounding grassy knolls. I want to walk over and rub my hand over his soft nose and hug his neck, but I am afraid that I will begin to blubber roundly in these open spaces, strangers seeing my breaking heart.

What is happening to me? I am crying on a street corner feeling such overwhelming pain for this poor, beautiful animal that cannot be free. I force myself to move on.

A few minutes later I am on the physical therapy table. Shmuel says, "Your body is in such pain today. What has happened?"

How can I say . . . *I saw a horse. . . and he looked so sad?*

"Life." I say. "Just my life."

Foods of Love

Not long ago, I heard someone say that nostalgia is the foods of your childhood. I agree. When I think back to my childhood, I think about my grandmother's table and my mother's outstanding culinary creations. My grandmother never wrote down a recipe. My mother, I assume, had to watch her as she cooked in order to make sure her favorites were not lost. My mother did keep a recipe file, but like her mother, she kept in her head the recipes for many of the ethnic foods that I love and which are now lost to me. She also did a funny thing. On some of her recipe cards she wrote down the name of the person who gave it to her. I do that, too. But, on the recipes I gave her, she wrote my whole name. Sheila Weinstein. And on her mother's, she wrote Fannie Epstein and under it (Mother). I know she didn't know any other Sheilas and certainly no other Fannie Epsteins. One of the things I'd ask her about if I could.

My children don't like many of the foods I loved when I was growing up, like borscht, gefilte fish (as long as I didn't have to stay around while it was cooking), and herring in sour cream. So, I set about creating foods for them that would become their nostalgia.

I loved feeding my family and hearing their yums. But, I also took on the chin a few yuks while I was learning to create good food. In that regard, I once made a recipe I copied from a magazine. It was called Yam Combo. Thinking back, I can't imagine why I wanted to cook such a thing. It even sounds disgusting. *Pieces of yam wrapped with chicken livers.* It will remain forever in my memory because my two-year-old daughter, who we called Little Lizzie then, took a bite of it and threw up on the table. My husband made some wisecrack, which I don't remember.

The next time I searched my recipe box for something to make for dinner, I found that recipe with a little * on it. And under it a note to me from my husband. It said: "Lizzie threw this one up." I have searched a long time for that recipe card and am convinced that someone threw it out to make certain it never made the table again.

I did a lot better for that sweet child after that. Some of her confessed favorites are: meatloaf, mashed potatoes, and tiny peas; spaghetti and meatballs; fried chicken; macaroni salad with tuna fish; and my sour cream coffee cake. She even fondly remembers the artery-clogging chicken fat smeared on a piece of rye bread with chicken cracklings I introduced to my kids before I cleaned up our eating act.

For my daughter Rachel, it is salade niçoise, tuna melts, French toast made with Challah, macaroni and cheese, fried bologna sandwiches, and best of all, she says, Campbell's tomato soup with a grilled cheese sandwich. And for my son, Bruce, who leans to the sweet side of life, chocolate-chip brownies, chocolate-chip cookies, peanut butter Rice Krispie treats with chocolate icing, and his teddy bear birthday cake, which, last year at the age of forty-five he asked me to make again. I had to paste together the soft and tattered recipe, now over forty years old.

My sweet husband never complained about anything I cooked for him, even the yam combo. He was the world's most accepting man. But, he would never let me make his birthday cake. He insisted on doing it himself. He had a recipe for a Pithivier, a round, buttery, French puff pastry tart filled with a delicate almond cream. It was a complicated recipe, but the most incredible thing about it was the way it looked. George, with his steady surgeon's hand, carved the top in a scallop design, which after baking was raised and shiny and crackling brown. It was the most delectable dessert we ever tasted. And every year at his birthday, we remember the Pithivier. Though none of us wants to try to duplicate it, the memory is still delicious.

It is rare for all my children and me to be together these days. We are scattered around the country. But there is one holiday we always count on to gather around a table: Thanksgiving. It's been different since I moved to New York. In my small kitchen and a dining room replaced by my piano, it has been a test of endurance to cook our traditional feast and serve it. One year, I put a tablecloth on a massage table and used that for a sideboard. Another year, I used the piano lid, covered with blankets and tablecloths. Another year, I just despaired of all the work and no room to do it in . . . so I took everyone to a restaurant. But we all missed the taste of my turkey and stuffing, so I ended up making our traditional feast the next night: roast turkey; bread stuffing; cranberry sauce with cassis and orange liqueur; mashed potatoes; green beans with mushrooms, garlic, bread crumbs, and Parmesan cheese; Southern corn casserole; apple pie; and chocolate pecan pie.

What is always missing, however, is George's role in the cooking of our feast. Every year he created his own delicious sauce for the turkey. He would not allow us to call it *gravy*. It was much more a masterpiece than that, replete with red wine and secret seasonings, and his skilled and patient hand. I've had to fill in for him these last Thanksgivings. And what I make is most definitely no masterpiece, but simply gravy.

No matter when we gather, what we do, besides talk at the same time, is eat. We take a break from eating healthy and let nostalgia have its way with us. Breakfast is easy in New York City. I go to one of our most famous shops, which happens to be next door to me . . . and get bagels, cream cheeses of all kinds, lox, plenty of Danish, and good coffee. For lunch and dinner, when we don't dine out, I cook what they desire most. There is still nothing better than to serve their favorite foods and once again hear the yums of contentment. No more yuks. I learned my lessons well.

At those times, seeing their beautiful faces, I am filled with gratitude for my family . . . together again, holding tightly to each other around the table, our hearts and souls fed, healed a little bit more, prepared for going out and away again, and looking forward to the next time we can enjoy together our particular foods of love.

Counterpoint

Counterpoint: the art and science of combining in a single texture two or more simultaneous melodic lines, each with a rhythmic life of its own.

Joseph Machlis, *The Enjoyment of Music*

I am now into my fifth year of living without my husband. Every experience of every day . . . some excruciatingly painful . . . some joyful . . . has been a new opportunity to learn more about myself . . . to watch myself at work and play . . . to see evidence of my own personal growth and maturity, which has nothing to do with my age. Except for the force of memory, it's almost hard to conjure the me that existed before George's diagnosis of dementia. I am living a life that I created for myself. And it is a happy one in the main. But the counterpoint in the music of my life is that George is dying in bits and pieces and I have to watch.

I am afraid that I have engaged in more than Joan Didion's *Year of Magical Thinking.* I have had seven years of it and, until my most recent visit to my husband, I still held some hope that a mystical power would suddenly fill the holes in George's brain and he would be healed. I didn't keep any of his clothes. I sent them all to wherever he was living because he would need to choose what to wear before he called me to ask where I'd been for so long and to come and get him.

In the days following his diagnosis, we used to sit together in our bedroom after dinner. He was still capable of speaking and, in hopes of helping him extend the time before the disease would no longer allow it, I suggested we read to each other each night. As he'd begin, I would move out of my chair, step behind him, and smooth down his soft, silver hair and then lightly move my hands over the crown of his head, over the parts of his brain that the disease had aimed for. I'd been into all kinds of New Age thought and practices and had taken courses in Reiki, a Japanese technique that is supposed to reduce stress and encourage healing. One conjures the life force of the universe which then flows through the hands to do the healing.

And so I stood, night after night, my hands on George's head, my eyes closed, trying to connect to that healing life force. Daily I watched for signs that it was working. I asked him questions. I monitored his behavior. I didn't give up until the day he told me he wanted to move into an assisted living facility without me. George had never wanted me out of his sight, let alone to live without me. According to his doctor, that was added proof that the disease was progressing, producing more emotional distancing.

The journey of his illness has taken George to a specialized care facility in California. Because I do not see him daily, my bimonthly visits are more poignant, as I can see more clearly the evidence of his continuing decline. And still, over these last few years, instead of accepting what I see, what I know intellectually, I have hoped and prayed, even laid hands on again, visualizing his now vacant eyes, clear and bright, his unsteady gait, strong and directed, his nonexistent speech restored and his soft deep voice suddenly telling me, as he takes my hand, how much he's missed me and that he's well again and please, can we go home. Only on my visit to him a month ago did that magical thinking finally bump up hard against the truth that he does not know or care that I am there—or not there.

Last year, I contracted some horrible virus that laid me low the entire winter so that I couldn't visit George for seven months. When I saw him again, the change in him was so devastating that I came home and soon found myself in a deep depression. It was then that I began to do some major work on myself to truly accept the reality of his illness. From the dark place into which I had fallen came the understanding that I was still carrying George's life in myself. I had lived his life for so many of our years together; but once we parted, I was certain that that was over. Apparently, I was still very much attached. And to save myself I would have to detach . . . to see him . . . but not take him in. To finally feel in my heart and soul that his journey was his. And mine was mine. And never the twain would meet . . . should meet . . . nor ever really had met.

I believe in the power of ritual, especially when it is one that I create for myself. I need one to help me along. Our forty-ninth wedding anniversary day comes. I buy myself two dozen roses of all colors. I wait for them to lose their bloom, then gently remove all the petals and place them in a beautiful crystal bowl. I write a thank-you letter to George and wait for the evening breeze from the river that swirls around the corner of my building at sunset. I open a window that faces a small garden, far below me, and gently throw handfuls of the petals into the wind . . . "My darling, George. My heart is filled with grief for the beauty of the life that was ours and the promise of the life that will never be . . . for the sweet touch of your gentle hand on my hair and your loving kiss and handsome face that shone with joy when I entered the room. And although you are still with us, for the impossibility of saying, though I must, farewell, love of my life, farewell."

Gradually the depression lifts. When it is time for me to visit George again, I am fearful that seeing him will cause me to fall into another one. I don't know if I can put into practice all that I have learned . . . if the ritual of detaching has etched its way into my heart. But I know that if I cannot find a way to see him without it destroying my ability to function well in my own life, then I might never be able to visit him again. That is abhorrent and guilt-provoking; but I have to consider the possibility.

In a session about this concern, my therapist suggests that perhaps when George and I are together, I could visualize putting up an invisible and impenetrable shield to keep myself separate from him. I conjure an old toothpaste ad for Colgate with Gardol, an invisible wall that wouldn't let any of the "bad stuff" through. I think it is a wonderful idea; but I am not sure if I can do it. I will only know by going to see George and watching myself closely as I move through our visit together.

After the session, as I sit pondering our conversation, I suddenly feel a rush of compassion for myself and for the pain that is still a part of my life and even for the reality that I might have to choose never to see George again if it would cost me my own life. And then, suddenly, I experience something grand and glorious . . . an inner shift in my experience from compassion to the reality of my personal power and truth. I *know* that I am strong enough to do anything I want to do. I *can* put my feelings in a place that will not unhinge me when I see George as he is now or when memories of him blindside me. I can separate my life from his because I *have* to . . . to save *me*.

I go to see George. It is difficult. I think of the rose petals. I don't remember the invisible shield. But, for whatever reason, I fully feel the separation of our paths. I return to New York and do not succumb to depression.

And I come to know this: There is something terrible about having to see George so desperately ill. But, that he is still living is also perversely comforting. I can still see him. I can see his face, his body, and his gentle hands I have loved for so long. Realizing the truth that we are no longer a single texture . . . if in fact we ever were . . . or if any two persons ever can be . . . but that each of us must continue to move with the rhythms of our own lives . . . is an ongoing effort. I cannot deny my sometimes desperate feelings when I am called in the middle of the night to hear that he has been taken to the hospital emergency room or, as on Thanksgiving day last, when my family was around me and I felt such joy in the now rare sound of all their happy voices . . . to receive a call saying that George was exhibiting signs of pain most likely caused by the recurrence of his cancer. I cannot run. I have to sit and listen, to make certain that he is being well-tended. And once I am certain, then my task remains to move into the room with the happy voices and add mine to theirs.

Broken Things

*I*t slips from my hand onto the tile floor . . . my treasured little crystal glass, a Scottish wildflower etched into its side. I grope the air as it tumbles and splinters.

"Don't cry over spilt milk," my mother said after anything but spilt milk.

Or "Don't cry over anything that money can replace."

I cry the green journey to the Scottish Highlands with George.

My chambered nautilus slides from its perch and smashes into an impossible puzzle. I bend and pick at the many bits of its pearl carapace and place them in my hand.

Treasures broken.

Like the bone of my life.

I cry for my little lost things.

I cry for me.

I am the fragile glass and the shell.

I sit with the pieces of my nautilus and imagine that tiny brave creature, growing, inching ever forward, sealing its former home, moving into a larger chamber . . . and the next . . . and the next . . . always toward the light.

I am the being whose skeletal life is larger. . . stronger with each space I leave behind me, hungry for each space before me in which to grow and become more of what I am meant to be.

Dancing in the Bathroom

The clock reads 4:30 a.m. Long, restful sleep eludes me once more. I lie in the dark, Pooh loudly snoring his doggy sleep, his little body pressed into my side. Sweet contentment.

I listen to the rain spattering the windows. I shift my position. My body hurts. A hot bath. I slip out of bed and into the bathroom and turn on the water, take off my nightgown, and raise the shade to look out at the city, alive with light and morning clatter.

I go back into the bedroom and tune in the Big Band Swing channel. Maybe if I move . . . dance a little . . . free these joints. In the dark, I stomp and swing my arms to the jazzy tune, laughing as I catch sight of myself in the mirror . . . the arthritic jitterbug.

The music changes. Slow now . . . "Dream . . . when you're feeling blue. Dream . . . that's the thing to do." And I sway, eyes closed, slow dancing, my arms wrapped around someone, no name, no face . . . his arms enfolding me. "Just let the smoke rings rise in the air . . . You'll find your share of memories there . . . so . . . dream . . ." And I dream and I dance as my man allows me to cry the blessing of being held again.

"Please . . . please, God . . . let me be touched just once more . . . by someone I love."

The Winter Season

I *have just returned from my early-morning* walk around the reservoir in Central Park. It is a beautiful sunny day, unseasonably warm for mid-November. Yesterday's furious wind and rain felled the last leaves on the trees and I was sad to see their stark outlines forecasting the onset of winter.

But then again, snow will soon cover those branches and add another kind of beauty to brighten my walks, and inevitably the trees will bud once more for the return of spring. And so it goes. But, not with us humans.

In a few months, I will celebrate my seventieth birthday, and I am more than aware that I do not have the opportunity to return to my spring, or summer, or autumn. Each season of my life is finite. And that fact leaves me open to muse on aging into the snowy beauty of my own personal winter.

A few days ago, one of my dearest friends, Jerry, called from her home in Texas. Ours is a long friendship. We wheeled strollers together when we lived in Brooklyn while our husbands were in training.

"I really can't believe that I'm going to be seventy . . . and I'll finally catch up to you," I laughed. "We are so . . . ooo . . ."

She interrupted, and in her fine Texas drawl said, "You don't have to say the word, honey. I know. And the worst of it is what the newspapers will say about you."

"The newspapers? What do you mean?"

"Well, if you cross the street and get hit by a bus, the newspaper article's gonna say: 'An elderly lady was crossing the street.'"

"Gee thanks," I said. "That makes me feel a lot better."

"Aw, darlin'. Don't worry. Be happy. Forget about the number."

But, I haven't.

The emotional aspect of realizing that I am closer to the end than the beginning is somewhat anxiety provoking. The fact that I have less ahead than behind makes me acutely aware that this is my last opportunity to really live this life I am given. And that makes it an imperative for me to define and refine what is important for me.

I've been aging since I was born, so actually what I'm doing is nothing that I haven't been doing. It's just that this late period demands more from me in terms of fortitude, good humor, and acceptance. My body has given me wonderful years and is now asking me to pay it back by lovingly tending its aches and pains and keeping it strong. And that, I am doing.

On certain days, when my knees ache, my back hurts, and I can't remember what I ate for dinner the night before or the name of my next-door neighbor, I am quite aware that I am no longer sixteen . . . although I seem to remain that young in my head. But unlike that teen, I'm gulping vitamins and regularly testing the health of my bones and breasts. The days of my youth, when the world smelled like lilacs, are over and my personal world is more like eucalyptus and menthol as I rub potions and unguents into my ailing joints.

Could I write a laundry list of complaints? Oh, boy . . . could I! The pains, the worries, the flights into the what-ifs and uh-ohs of tomorrow! The sad fact that I still acutely feel the loss of my husband and the care and love we could have given each other at this precarious time of life. But dwelling on the negatives only makes me feel worse. How I live and what I believe about this time of life will either leave me mired in its ditches and difficulties or help me squeeze all the joy and wonder and goodness from the time that is left to me.

I was always afraid I'd get to the end of my days and see in the mirror an old woman who hadn't lived her own life. And so I intend that the fewer years left than lived will continue to be rich with experience and possibility. I feel now squarely centered in my bed, taking charge of my life as much as anyone can, considering the fates. I am most definitely not the frightened, anxious woman I was when this journey alone began, and I've worked hard at getting to the place where I could say that honestly. And, more, I have had a taste . . . or rather a feast . . . of independence and it has made me desirous of living independently for the rest of my days . . . if I can.

When I was a very young girl—and sadly, into womanhood—insecure and searching for a feeling of safety, I used to try to figure out what was a sure thing. What could I believe in that would never let me down? It took me a long time to understand that safety and security lie *within me* and the only sure thing is that everything is in a constant state of flux. I have become, if not comfortable, at least reconciled with living with uncertainty as I find more and more security within.

So I can move forward and fill in the gaps. Learn more. Read more. Go where I want to go within my own possibilities. Be with the people I love and who love me; keep on writing and playing the piano; tend my spiritual life; be of service to others; guard my solitude where I am never lonely or in pain, angry, or unhappy; be in nature; eat well; and always . . . always . . . have something wonderful planned for tomorrow. It doesn't have to be a big thing. Just something I want to do . . . finishing a piece of writing or starting to learn a new piece of music, seeing the new exhibit at the Metropolitan Museum, having lunch with a friend . . . or baking a cake. I love cake.

And, above all, to be grateful for what I have here and now.

My recipe for happy living.

And, for the days after the tomorrows, I have a list . . . not a long one . . . of things I would still like to do or have happen to me. I'd like to publish all my good writing. I'd like to learn to play the harp. I'd like to be held in the arms of a fabulous male dancer and learn the tango without falling on my behind or destroying what's left of my knees. I'd like to go to Ireland and Greece. And dine again in Paris. And, yes, I would like to love again and be loved. I don't think I would ever want to marry again. Love would be enough.

I have realized, as I go about my life and later years, that my children and grandchildren are watching me closely. I didn't have a maternal role model to watch as she aged. My mother died when I was in my early thirties. I have had to be my own guide. And that's okay. I'm a do-it-myselfer anyway. But, what I would like to model for myself first, and then for all of them as I continue on, is personal courage, fortitude, wisdom, and the ability to fall down and get up again. I have learned much from all the living. I have taken in, spit out, adjusted, readjusted, fallen apart, and put myself together again—and the positives of all of that are that I now feel able to be of service to them should they need what I have to offer.

I know that I cannot know the answers to the big questions. But over the years, I have formulated my own philosophy that has allowed me, hopefully, to age with grace. I believe that my life has a purpose and that I was sent here to find out exactly what that is. I believe that I have an inward compass that points me due north, and by that I mean toward giving the best that is in me each and every day no matter what happens. I believe strongly that what I think about I will draw to me and, therefore, I try to make my thoughts and wishes good ones. I fail a lot; but I keep trying. And of course, I know that one day my body will die; although I believe my soul will live on. Meantime, I continue to try to find meaning in this grand and glorious, painful and unpredictable, sad, happy, and at times, searingly grief-filled life. I live a lot in my mind. I always find music there and inspiring words. They lift me above what my eyes see.

When my aging has come to its end, I don't know if I will go "gentle into that good night" or "rage, rage against the dying of the light . . ." to paraphrase Dylan Thomas. I tend to believe it will be the latter. Because I think I will always feel like I have more to do, and besides, I like it here. But, who knows? I have yet to write the end of the story. And so, I intend to continue forward, my glass raised, reciting the wonderful French toast *"Pour la vie . . . comme il vient!"* To life as it comes.

They're Writing Songs of Love, But Not For Me

I am standing in Kate's Paperie, one of my favorite stores in New York City. I look at pens, cards, and day planners, and choose a box of notes, hand-engraved with little dragonflies.

Music plays overhead. I hum along. I stop in front of shelves of colorful wrappings and ribbons. A new song begins. After the first three notes, I know what it is . . . the one George and I chose when we were teens to be our song. "Our Love is Here to Stay."

Quickly the colorful ribbons and papers blur. I lean against the wall and listen until the song ends. Maybe it's a sign. Maybe George is sending me a message . . . telling me he is with me.

Tears drop onto my cheeks. I find a tissue and cover my face, pretending to sneeze. Someone might see and ask if I'm okay. It happens, even in New York. I don't want to tell them . . . no, I'm not okay. I just heard a love song that was once meant for me. Maybe "Our Love is Here to Stay" but my love is not.

It is in that moment that I fully realize that I will most likely not have another love in my life. That love songs will never again be written for me.

And I will survive.

Ten Cents a Dance

Yes. I will survive. Yes, I will continue to seek my life and my joy in places to which I am drawn by desire or interest or curiosity. But the loss of my love has taken away one of the greatest things that passed between us. Touch. I can wish to be touched by someone I love, as I did dancing in the bathroom; but wishing will not make it so. In the days following the realization in Kate's Paperie that I will not be loved or be in love again something has been working on me, through me . . . something I can't put my finger on but which knows how to get my attention. In a song . . . a song that keeps twirling in my head. A song that dates from before my birth. But the feelings it speaks to are timeless. "Ten Cents a Dance." Ruth Etting, a songstress in the 1930s, stopped the Rogers and Hart show, *Simple Simon*, singing that song. It's about a woman working in a ballroom. Anyone can dance with her if they pay the requisite ten cents.

But why *that* song? And why won't it leave me? I think and think, and then when I'm not thinking, I know.

It's not about the poor beleaguered woman. It's not about the dance. It's about the human need to feel the closeness of another human body. Ultimately, it's about the healing beauty of the human touch. I am denied the exquisite joy of being touched by the man I love, his gentle hand on my hair, my shoulders, my arms . . . and at night the contentment I felt as it ran along the curve of my body as I lay on my side. And his voice that whispered in the silence, "You are so beautiful. You'll never know how much I love you."

Suddenly, no voice. No sweet touch.

Yes, the love of my life is still here, physically, but his mind has retreated to a place where I cannot follow. I so long for times that can never come again, that I still find myself trying to make them happen. When I go to see George, I put on music and encourage him to dance with me. I put his arm around my waist and take his other hand in mine and draw him to me. And I am once again close to the same body that held me and stroked me and that offered me a momentary sense of safety. But it only makes me want to scream out my longing, my anger, my rage. Because the essence of him is not there. What made that love between us, what was under the glorious gentle touch is gone. And I am holding onto a dream as I once did of my long dead mother, running to her, shouting, "Oh, you came back for my birthday," and throwing my arms around her neck only to find . . . nothing but air.

And so, now I have to pay for the privilege of touch. No longer ten cents a dance. More like eighty-five dollars an hour. But on some days I'd pay anything. Not for a dance, but for the hands-on experience of a body worker. I go to a masseuse, a kind and gentle woman. Her touch is lovely, different to be sure, but comforting. Then, one day, I choose a man, a highly recommended massage therapist. And as I lay on his table, his hands searching my body, not with love but with a calming firmness that seeks out the places where loneliness has gathered into knots of pain, my tears flow silently. I have all I can do not to reach up and take his hands in mine and say, "Oh, thank you, thank you, thank you."

Legacy

I *am introduced to a woman by a mutual*
friend. We enjoy each other's company and find that
we have many common interests. One day at lunch she
mentions that she is preparing an Ethical Will. She says it is
becoming more and more popular in the Jewish religion, to
which she has converted and into which I was born. I have
never heard of an Ethical Will. What I learn is that, in essence,
it is a statement of a person's beliefs about themselves . . .
a marker of ones thoughts and feelings about anything and
everything one cares to make known and to leave as a personal
legacy.

After our discussion, I realize that I actually did such a
thing about ten years ago without giving it a name. It was
a response to a request from my daughter Rachel. She said,
"Mom, if you were not available to me anymore . . ." (It was
too hard for her to say "If you were to die") "what are some
of the things you would want me to know? I hear your voice
in my head all the time, but I want some specifics . . . just in
case."

It was an interesting and also a challenging request and I immediately went to my computer to think with my hands about her question. After some time spent trying to define myself, I decided just to close my eyes and write from my heart.

As I think back, I realize Rachel was asking me to do something important. To tell her who I am and what I stand for . . . even though as Gandhi said, "My life is my message." I want my children to know me, as much as it is possible to know anyone other than ourselves . . . and even that process is a constant challenge. And so, I am grateful to my daughter for asking and for the privilege of setting down my thoughts for her . . . and for myself as well.

I can't dictate or predict what my personal legacy will be. I hope it will be of a life lived honorably and completely. If words can embody the spirit of me and what I believe, then I think those I wrote to my daughter are the ones I would still choose . . . as it is for me now as it was then.

And so, I include my letter to her here, at the end.

May 1, 1996

My darling Rachel,

During your recent visit, you asked me to tell you things I want you to know if ever you and I would not be able to communicate on this plane. It is an interesting and difficult request for me to fulfill. Because although my soul and spirit will live on in another dimension, I am sure, earthly thoughts that I will be leaving behind the best of what I am, and that is you, make me sad to contemplate my own mortality.

I purposely did not think through what I am about to set down because I wanted it to come straight from my heart. So, my daughter, this is what I want you to know:

That love is the most important thing to give and to receive.

That you should marry your best friend.

That you should feel treasured, respected, and honored by him, forever.

That you should accord him the same.

That maintaining close family ties is a worthy goal, but one which may not be possible to attain.

That good friends mean a healthy life.

That what we put into our bodies tells us what value we place on our being.

That material goods are necessary and make life easier.

That without a deep sense of self-worth and wholeness they will never be enough.

That your intelligence, love, insight, and compassion are a blessing to those around you.

That your gentle heart will sometimes feel bruised and shaken.

That, nonetheless, you must continue to love and help and trust that all will be well, because it will.

That each choice you make will lead you further down the path to your true self, whether or not the outcome is what you desire.

148

That you should forgive yourself what you consider mistakes, and know that we do the very best we can with what we know at the time.

That you must listen to the voice within you. It will guide and protect you.

That dreaming is good.

That making your dreams come true is even better.

That who you are is more important than what you choose as work.

That you can see a candle better in the dark.

That being down teaches more than being up.

That withdrawal from the world is necessary at times to bring you back to your self.

That feeding your soul with sounds, tastes, scents, sights, and touches is an everyday imperative.

That it is good to love an animal.

That you should seek and honor the Divine presence in everything and everyone.

That, nevertheless, there are toxic people from whom you must separate yourself.

That everyone and everything you meet is part of your earthly lesson plan.

That you must be open to life and all it will bring you, learning from each and every sadness and gladness, clinging to neither because they will change.

That you must live honorably and ethically.

That your word is your sacred promise.

That you must give solely from the love in your heart, asking for nothing in return.

That despite all the miseries you see around you and experience yourself, there is a unifier, a spirit of goodness, compassion, and love that is the center of life.

That the highest achievement we can aspire to is to know that.

That prayer is healing.

That there are angels in human form.

That you are one of them.

That I have loved you more than myself.

That I have tried to give you the best I have to give.

That if I have succeeded, you know that you have everything inside you that you need to make it through.

That when we can no longer speak in words, you need only open your heart and I will hear it, and lift your beautiful face, and I will kiss it.

That we will always be together.

With my heart full of love and gratitude for all that you are, my Rachel,

> *I am your Mother, forever.*

Dusk

I stand at the living room window, glass of wine in hand. I have had a good day of writing. It is dusk, a beautiful, soft, gray-apricot dusk on a cold January day. A delicious meal I have created to my taste is in the making. My turkey/mushroom burgers are frying in the pan. Standing by in a glass bowl is my salad with its Ranch dressing the commercial made me want so badly. Favorite music is playing . . . the sound track of *The Legend of 1900*, a voluptuous movie that has held me in its thrall, music by Ennio Morricone, a man with soul. I must remember to buy his other works.

I look out at the East River and the bridge to Randall's Island, the pink reflection of its lights zigzagging in the water below. And I am suddenly aware that I am wildly happy. I breathe in deeply, this happiness, this dusk, this brief, heart breakingly beautiful time before the velvet cover of night. I breathe in my life . . . a life that is solely mine. Never before, not as a child, adult, wife, or mother have I felt myself so firmly within my skin . . . looking out with eyes that have watched me create the beauty of my life, that see what lies before me, anticipating the time I have here on earth to do what is in me to do.

I am at the other end now . . . squarely in the center of my bed.

I am alone. I am content. I am grateful.

I am hungry.

The Telephone Rings

*I*t is the hospice nurse in California. George has suddenly declined. He is not able to walk. A hospital bed and wheelchair have been ordered. He is not eating on his own; but being fed. He has lost weight. There is nothing imminent but it is certain that he has entered a new phase of his disease.

I will be there I say. I just cannot come until my son is married next week.

Hold on, my darling George. Please, please wait . . . until I can kiss you and say goodbye.

About the Author

*S*heila weinstein grew up in New Jersey. She met her future husband when she was eleven years old and married him when she was twenty and in her senior year at Barnard College in New York City. After graduating with a degree in French, she worked at the United Nations for two years until their son was born. They moved around the country to pursue her husband's professional goals as an ophthalmologist. With the addition of their two daughters, Sheila focused full time on being a wife and mother.

The family traveled around the world and even lived in Algeria for several months when her husband worked at the Beni Messous Hospital. When they returned to the U.S. and moved to Texas, Sheila decided to pursue her great love of the piano and obtained a Master's Degree in Piano Performance at Trinity University in San Antonio. After ten years, the family returned to the East and settled in Morgantown, West Virginia, where Sheila taught piano at the Creative Arts Center of West Virginia University and then privately in their home.

In the early 1990s, Sheila gave up teaching piano to pursue writing seriously. In 1995, Sheila and her husband moved again, this time to Florida, where he opened a private practice in ophthalmology. In 1999, her husband was diagnosed with dementia. After forty-two years of marriage, she had to learn how to live without the support of the love of her life.

Sheila now lives in New York City, where she is a docent at Carnegie Hall, taking visitors on tours every Monday. She has given piano concerts in her home and, in September 2008, was privileged to be part of a group of musicians who performed at Carnegie Hall's Weill Recital Hall.

She especially enjoys spending time with family and friends; her special dog, Pooh; walking in Central Park; eating dark chocolate; cooking; and baking for her doormen and anyone else who loves cookies and cakes. Sheila loves going to the theatre, museums, and concerts; learning new piano pieces; reading; starting new writing projects; and watching sunsets from her bedroom window and the sunrise over the East River.